Small Group Teaching

Tutorials, seminars and beyond

Kate Exley and Reg Dennick

RoutledgeFalmer
Taylor & Francis Group

LONDON AND NEW YORK

First published 2004 by RoutledgeFalmer
2 Park Square, Milton Park, Abingdon, OX14 4RN

Simultaneously published in the USA and Canada
by RoutledgeFalmer
270 Madison Ave, New York, NY 10016

Reprinted 2005

RoutledgeFalmer is an imprint of the Taylor & Francis Group

© 2004 Kate Exley and Reg Dennick

Typeset in Perpetua and Bell Gothic by Graphicraft Limited, Hong Kong
Printed and bound in Great Britain by TJ International Ltd, Padstow, Cornwall

Key Guides for Effective Teaching in Higher Education web resource

The Key Guides for Effective Teaching in Higher Education Series provides
guidance and advice for those looking to improve their teaching and learning.
It is accompanied by a useful website which features brand new supplemen-
tary material, including How Students Learn, a guide written by Professor
George Brown which provides outlines and commentaries on theories of
learning and their implications for teaching practice.

Visit the website at: www.routledgefalmer.com/series/KGETHE

The RoutledgeFalmer website also features a wide range of books for
lecturers and higher education professionals.

British Library Cataloguing in Publication Data
A catalogue record for this book is available from the British Library

Library of Congress Cataloging in Publication Data
Exley, Kate, 1964–
    Small group teaching / Kate Exley and Reg Dennick.
        p. cm. – (Effective teaching in higher education)
    Includes bibliographical references and index.
        1. College teaching.   2. Group work in education.
    3. Small groups.   I. Dennick, Reg, 1949–   II. Title.
    III. Series.
    LB2331.E937   2004
    378.1′795–dc22   2003017437

ISBN 0–415–30717–1 (pbk)
ISBN 0–415–30716–3 (hbk)

Contents

Illustrations

Figures

Tables

Series preface

This series of books grew out of discussions with new lecturers and part-time teachers in universities and colleges who were keen to develop their teaching skills. However, experienced colleagues may also enjoy and find merit in the books, particularly the discussions about current issues that are impacting on teaching and learning in further education (FE) and higher education (HE) (e.g. Widening Participation, disability legislation and the integration of Communication and Information Technology (C&IT) in teaching).

New lecturers may be required by their institutions to take part in teaching development programmes. This frequently involves attending workshops, investigating teaching through mini-projects and reflecting on their practice. Many teaching programmes ask participants to develop their own teaching portfolios and to provide evidence of their developing skills and understanding. Scholarship of teaching is usually an important aspect of the teaching portfolio. New teachers can be asked to consider their own approach to teaching in relation to the wider literature, research findings and theory of teaching and learning. However, when people are beginning their teaching careers, a much more pressing need may be to design and deliver an effective teaching session for tomorrow. Hence the intention of this series is to provide a complementary mix of very practical teaching tips and guidance together with a strong basis and clear rationale for their use.

In many institutions the numbers of part-time and occasional teachers actually outnumber the full-time staff. Yet the provision of formal training and development for part-time teachers is more sporadic and variable across the sector. As a result this diverse group of educators can feel isolated and left out of the updating and support offered to their full-time counterparts. At no time has there been so many part-time teachers involved in the design and delivery of courses, the support and guidance of students and the monitoring and assessment of learning. The group includes the thousands of postgraduate students who work as lab demonstrators, problem class tutors, project supervisors and class teachers. The group includes clinicians, lawyers and professionals who contribute their specialist knowledge and skills to enrich the learning experience for many vocational and professional course students. The group also includes the many hourly paid and jobbing tutors who have helped full-time staff cope with the expansion and diversification of HE and FE.

Universities sometimes struggle to know how many part-time staff they employ to teach and as a group, occasional teachers are notoriously difficult to systematically contact through university and college communication systems. Part-time and occasional teachers often have other roles and responsibilities and teaching is a small but important part of what they do day to day. Many part-time tutors would not expect to undertake the full range of teaching activities of full-time staff but may well do lots of tutoring or lots of class teaching but never lecture or supervise (or vice versa). So the series provides short practical books focusing very squarely on different teaching roles and activities. The first four books published are

- *Small Group Teaching*
- *Giving a Lecture: From Presenting to Teaching*
- *Assessing Students' Written Work*
- *Using C&IT to Support Teaching*

The books are all very practical with detailed discussion of teaching techniques and methods but they are based upon educational theory and research findings. Articles are referenced, further readings and related web sites are given and workers in the field are quoted and acknowledged. To this end Professor George Brown has been commissioned to produce an associated web-based guide on Student Learning which can be freely accessed by readers to accompany the books and provide a substantial foundation for the teaching and assessment practices discussed and recommended in the texts. The URL for this site is: www.routledgefalmer.com/series/KGETHE

There is much enthusiasm and support here too for the excellent work currently being carried out by the Learning and Teaching Support Networks (LTSN) within discipline groupings (indeed individual LTSN centres are suggested as sources of further information throughout these volumes). The need to provide part-time tutors with the realistic connections with their own disciplines is keenly felt by all the authors in the series and 'how it might work in your department' examples are given at the end of many of the activity based chapters. However, there is no doubt some merit in sharing teaching developments across the boundaries of discipline, culture and country as many of the problems in the tertiary education sector are themselves widely shared.

UNDERLYING THEMES

The use of Computing and Information Technology (C&IT) to enrich student learning and to help manage the workload of teachers is a recurrent theme in the series. I acknowledge that not all teachers may yet have access to state-of-the-art teaching resources and facilities. However, the use of virtual learning environments, e-learning provision and audio-visual presentation media is becoming increasingly widespread in universities.

The books also acknowledge, and try to help new teachers respond to, the growing and changing nature of the student population. Students with non-traditional educational backgrounds, international students, students who have disabilities or special needs are encouraged through the government's widening participation agenda to take part in further and higher education. The books seek to advise teachers on current legislative requirements and guide on recommended good practice in teaching diverse groups of students.

These were our goals and I and my co-authors sincerely hope these volumes prove to be a helpful resource for colleagues, both new and experienced, in HE.

Kate Exley

Acknowledgements

The authors of this book gratefully acknowledge the support, input and encouragement that they have received from friends, colleagues and family. Particular thanks go to Richard Blackwell, the South East Regional Consultant for HEFCE and formally of the LTSN Generic Centre. Richard provided clear insight, critical conversations and constructive feedback during the writing of this book and its final drafts.

Special thanks must go to colleagues who have given helpful suggestions and feedback and told us about their small group teaching strategies from a wide range of discipline areas. The list is by no means exhaustive but does include Liz Barnett, Liz Sockett, Catherine Moore, Shake Seigel, Wyn Morgan, Stan Taylor, Paul Chin, Peter Davies, Jordi Vaquer-Fanes and Rachel Scudamore. A big thank you to Mike Exley for drawing the illustrations.

Sincere thanks too to Alison Foyle and Priyanka Pathak at Routledge-Falmer. Their knowledge of the process of writing and publishing and their understanding of authors' foibles made their help and guidance invaluable.

Chapter 1

The goals of small group teaching

WHAT IS SMALL GROUP TEACHING?

The heading of *Small Group Teaching* does include a wide variety of different kinds of classes in further and higher education, some of the most common being seminars, tutorials, workshops and problem based learning (PBL) meetings. A common feature of this kind of teaching is that the tutor works with a small group of students to discuss a given topic or a given problem. There are, however, other forms of small group teaching (SGT) which place much less emphasis on the presence of a tutor or teacher and seek to provide the students with a formalized opportunity for collaborative learning. These include tutor-less tutorials, self-help groups and learning sets.

These SGT methods require students (and tutor) to be present in the same room at the same time. There is also a growing interest in the use of 'virtual' SGT methods that use computing and information technology (C&IT) to bring students together. These include the use of closed email networks and intranet and internet discussion forums, which enable students and teachers to interact at a distance. The technology also means that discussions can take place over a longer timescale, with contributions to discussions being made over days rather than minutes.

There is one final category of SGT to mention here which blurs the boundary between small and large group teaching. A teacher may choose to organize and divide a larger group of students so that in fact they are working in a series of small groups. This is often referred to as syndic-ate working and allows the teacher to use many SGT approaches, even when the class size is large. This method is commonly observed in problem classes, group project work and practical classes. These four categories of SGT are summarized for you in Table 1.1.

TABLE 1.1 The four categories of small group teaching

Categories of small group teaching	Examples of small group approaches	Typical student numbers
Tutor-led SGT	Tutorials	4–12
	Seminars	10–25
	PBL groups	8–12
Student-led SGT	Tutor-less tutorials	4–8
	Learning sets	4–8
	Self-help groups	4–8
Virtual SGT	Virtual tutorials	4–12
	Email discussions	4 upwards
SGT in large groups	Syndicate work	10–100
	Problem classes	10–50
	Group practicals	10–100
	Workshops	10–40

THE SIZE OF THE SMALL GROUP?

There is a consensus that the optimum size for small group teaching, in general, is between five and eight per group and for tutor-led, tutorial type SGT a group of six is best (Booth 1996). When group membership falls below five, the diversity and variety of interpersonal interaction diminishes; with more than eight members, the contribution from some individuals will start to decline. Please see Chapter 2 for further discussion of the optimum conditions for SGT.

WHY USE SGT?

SGT is expensive, particularly in terms of human resources, yet it is widely used in higher education. In many institutions there has been a growth in student numbers without a corresponding increase in the numbers of people to teach them. This has put an obvious pressure on the viability of SGT, yet it remains an important and valued part of many university courses. This chapter considers why this is the case.

(Please consult Brown (2004) *How Students Learn*, the web guide accompanying this book series (www.routledgefalmer.com/series/KGETHE), for further consideration of the learning and process benefits of SGT.)

THE AIMS OF SGT

In a small group students can be encouraged to talk, think and share much more readily than in a larger group. Communication is at the heart of small group teaching of any kind and a crucial first step is the willingness of the students to speak to the tutor and to each other.

There is merit in making the core aims of SGT explicit to the students and to explain the value of 'talking' about what you are 'thinking' to others in terms of their personal and intellectual development.

CONTENT AND PROCESS

Here we present the view that discussion and other talking related activities can be crucial for the development of both the content focus and the process focus of a SGT session (Table 1.2). The take-home message is that in SGT the aim is not simply the transmission of content but the need to work with that content within a group situation.

During a class discussion the tutor can see students using two sets of overlapping skills. These are first the generic *process* orientated skills of discussion which include, for example, how the students are

TABLE 1.2 The contribution of discussion to both the content and the process foci of a SGT session

Process focus	Content focus
Personal and professional skills	Academic and intellectual skills
Communication skills ■ presenting ■ listening ■ responding ■ questioning	Deep learning
	Problem solving ■ diagnosing ■ theorizing ■ evaluating evidence ■ analysing / synthesizing
Personal development	
Reflective practice	Using the language of the discipline
Group working	Making an argument
Collaboration and learning from others	Defending a viewpoint
	Clarifying and understanding
	Exploring the rules of the 'discipline'

communicating with each other and we can assume that all students, no matter what their particular discipline, will practise these skills in a SGT session. Second, there are the *content* focused skills that are more closely associated with studying a particular discipline and discussing particular topics, for example critical analysis or constructing an argument. Specific academic skills may be so embedded in the nature of a discipline that the skills almost become the 'content' of that discipline, for example, diagnosing for a doctor, defending a viewpoint to the lawyer, making an argument to the philosopher etc. It is part of what defines the discipline. Table 1.2 aims to map some of the skills developed through discussion under these two foci of process and content. This is clearly not an exact science and it is possible to map some skills to both areas by considering skills at different levels of their development. A process skill may become specialized and more content focused when practised at a higher and more complex level in the same way as *talking* can become *debate*, which in turn can develop and can become *critical analysis*.

The aims of SGT can be described as follows:

- *The development of intellectual understanding:* by clarifying concepts and theories through discussion and accepting and seeing interrelationships and connections.
- *The development of intellectual and professional abilities:* by thinking and problem solving, e.g. analysing, evaluating evidence, logical reasoning and synthesizing.
- *The development of communication skills:* through discussion practising giving explanations, listening, questioning, presenting and defending a position and giving constructive feedback.
- *Personal growth:* by taking part in debate and discussion students can test their values and attitudes while developing self-esteem and self-confidence.
- *Professional growth*: through close and focused exchanges with teachers and peers in the discipline, students become aware of the models of thinking, the accepted standards and the values and ethics of the discipline or profession.
- *Support for independence:* by preparing for and taking part in small group teaching discussions and activities, students accept their personal responsibility for the progress and direction of their own learning.

4

■ *The development of group working skills:* working in a group gives an opportunity to practise a variety of group management skills and group roles including leadership, planning and organization, giving support and encouragement to others, setting tasks, monitoring progress.

■ *Reflective practice:* by reviewing and reflecting on their actions students can learn from their successes and failures and so develop their skills and understanding and plan future learning.

(adapted from Entwistle *et al.* 1992: 41)

DISCUSSION IN SGT

> If lecturers are characterised by the transmission of information to frequently passive receivers then SGT by comparison is about active interpersonal communication and the learning benefits that derive from this.
>
> (Dennick and Exley 1998: 6)

SGT allows learners to discuss ideas and concepts with fellow learners and teachers. Learners can be provoked into thinking deeply by challenging questions from peers and teacher. In terms of the learning domains of knowledge, skills and attitudes, SGT has a clear role in helping students to broaden and deepen their understanding, develop professional and key skills and gain insight into their attitudes, bias and prejudices.

SGT is also important when students are learning how to use their academic or intellectual skills within their chosen discipline, and to practise and hone their skills of application, analysis, synthesis and evaluation (Bloom 1956, 1964).

CONSTRUCTIVISM AND ACTIVE LEARNING

SGT processes can clearly support a 'constructive' approach to learning. Constructivism (Phillips 2000) has at its heart the view that individual students construct or build their own knowledge and understanding rather than simply acquiring it pre-packaged and ready-made. The knowledge that they build will depend on several factors including what they are formally taught, what they find out for themselves, what they share with their peers and tutor and the culture of their discipline and their

5

society in which they learn. The process of using and articulating ideas and concepts helps in the 'elaboration' of learning (Coles 1991). Similarly learning, which is contextualized in an active environment where ideas are discussed and challenged, is more likely to result in 'deep' level learning (Atherton 2002).

(Please consult Brown (2004) *How Students Learn*, the web guide accompanying this book series (www.routledgefalmer.com/series/KGETHE), for more information on constructivism and active learning.)

TAKING RESPONSIBILITY

SGT encourages students to take ownership of their own learning: it isn't done for them, they need to take responsibility for their own preparation and the way in which they conduct themselves during the class. Much small group teaching depends upon the active engagement of the students and calls for them to express their opinions and to respond to the ideas and views of others. The communication processes involved can be varied and complex. Students may need to negotiate and debate, they may need to explain their position or ask questions, they will be asked to give and receive feedback as well as developing oral presentation skills. Through these processes the students can develop attitudes of respect and tolerance towards other points of view and can even help others to learn.

TOWARDS PROFESSIONAL PRACTICE

SGT also initiates learners into 'reflective practice', which leads to the development of 'professional practice' as characterized by Donald Schön (1987). For our students, the aim of 'reflecting-in-action' is that they can move beyond simply applying previously mastered competencies in a mechanistic way. Graduating students should be able to use their professional knowledge and skills to select appropriate approaches when responding to new problems and situations. Students can be supported in SGT as they move towards professional practice and develop greater flexibility and responsiveness.

THE DEVELOPMENT OF SKILLS

When students are participating in SGT they have an opportunity to develop their communication skills and group working skills. Whether the classes are discursive or problem based, students will need to listen, explain, question, respond and, in some classes, present their work. In the past the development of such skills has been seen as a useful by-product of a main focus on knowledge attainment and gaining the intellectual skills discussed earlier. However, the report of the National Committee of Inquiry into Higher Education (Dearing 1997) recommended that the development of key skills (communication skills, numeracy, the use of information technology and learning how to learn) should be included in every degree programme. The Dearing report was in part a response to the views of many graduate employers that students were not encouraged to develop these skills during their courses. The view that new graduates knew an awful lot but still needed intensive and expensive training to operate effectively in the workplace was common. However, the Dearing report stressed that its recommendation was based on the notion that the attainment of key skills was necessary for life and not just for entering employment. Indeed, the report is strongly supportive of the need to equip students with the abilities to continue to learn independently and is in line with popular views on lifelong learning and continuing professional updating and development.

> Those leaving higher education will need to understand how to learn and how to manage their own learning and recognise that the process continues throughout life.
>
> (Dearing 1997: 134)

The report also said 'that clear descriptions of programmes should be developed so that students are able to compare different offerings and make sensible choices about the programmes they wish to take' (Dearing 1997: 134) (see Chapter 7 for further details).

In direct response to Dearing, the Quality Assurance Agency for Higher Education (QAA) established forty-seven subject working groups and asked them to produce benchmarking statements that describe the standards for degree programmes in their forty-seven different discipline areas. This was completed in March 2002. The benchmarking statements do not, in the main, specify a syllabus but attempt to indicate the intellectual, professional and key skills that a graduate should possess, giving key skills a prominent position in curriculum design. The QAA also, as part of its reformed quality review process, required institutions to produce programme specifications for all degree courses.

The programme specification should provide clear information about a course and make reference to the relevant subject benchmarking statement and indicate where in the programme students will gain the appropriate knowledge and skills.

When academics and programme leaders began to review their own programmes and courses in this light, many considered that the obvious teaching vehicle for the development of key skills was through SGT activities and forms of practical and project work. Therefore, many teachers are currently using SGT as a way of providing information and guidance on key skills and for giving opportunities for students to practise them. Key skills are increasingly being advertised as explicit learning outcomes of SGT classes.

Tutors may therefore need to plan their small group sessions with this in mind and consider how best to support communication skills and group working in their classes. Some SGT may also need to be assessed. For example, marks may be allocated for contribution to class discussion, teamworking or presentation skills (see Chapter 11 for further information).

STUDENTS SUPPORTING STUDENTS

One of the real benefits of SGT is that students are strongly encouraged to learn from each other as well as from the tutor. Indeed in some SGT sessions the tutor may not always be present. Students can be asked to share their views and help their peers to understand complex theories or explanations. This requires a degree of collaboration and free exchange not commonly found in other forms of teaching. The role of the tutor changes from being that of information giver to being one of facilitator and guide. The role of the students also changes from being one who is taught, to one who learns and helps their colleagues to learn. But with this increased involvement comes responsibility and there is no doubt that some students are able to take this better than others. The tutor may need to check that appropriate or correct information (depending on the topic and discipline) is being conveyed between students. The tutor may also need to underline the importance of points made by students, as their peers may not immediately value a contribution by another student as highly as one made by the tutor. For example, if a class includes student-led discussions or student presentations, the tutor may need to summarize and conclude at the end of the class to help ensure that the key points are heard by all.

If SGT includes activities such as peer tutoring, group managed projects or tasks, and self and peer monitoring, then the participating students are often called upon to think beyond what they have been given or taught. Such metacognitive learning has been shown (Boud 1995; Biggs 1999) to lead to deeper and more lasting understanding, so there are real benefits for the more able students in helping their less able or less experienced peers to learn.

> If I can teach something I know that I really understand it.
> (Postgraduate tutor in chemistry)

The benefits for the students' learning with help from their peers can also be very clear. An interesting investigation into improving student learning was carried out at the University of Bergen, Norway in the early 1990s. Additional training was provided for some students at the end of their first year, either in the form of a tutored revision programme or membership of a study group led by a second-year student. Both sets were assessed at the end of the year through an unseen written examination together with a third group of non-participating students, who were not given any additional training. The difference between the two training regimes was remarkable when compared with the non-participating group. The tutor-led programme produced only marginal improvements in the final examination performance, whereas the student-led study group not only had far fewer students failing the examination (6.5 per cent failed compared with 23 per cent in the non-participating group) but also the number of 'very good' marks rose to 48 per cent as compared with 26 per cent in the non-participating group (Raaheim 1991).

It is not clear why such dramatic results were observed. It might be that the student tutors were better able to pitch the level of help, or that the student learners felt more able to communicate with and ask questions of a peer rather than a tutor, but it does provide encouraging evidence for the effectiveness of students supporting students.

It is also important to recognize that the majority of students really enjoy collaborative learning and forms of group work. It is commonly found that when group projects run, other teachers can be heard to complain that the students are spending too much of their time and effort on their group projects at the expense of other classes. If students want to learn and enjoy the process, then they are much more likely to meet and go beyond the expectations of their tutors.

9

TEAMWORKING AND THE MULTIDISCIPLINARY GROUP

In asking students to work together and to collaborate in learning, we do more than ask them to share their views and exchange their ideas. We ask them to learn how to accommodate each other's beliefs and cultures. We invite them to approach topics from different starting points and to broaden their intellectual and personal horizons. This can be seen as a distinct goal of SGT especially when graduates will be expected to work in multidisciplinary teams in their future employment. For example, in medicine and engineering courses considerable effort has been made in incorporating mixed group teaching and problem based learning in the curriculum. In medicine, the small groups may include medics, nurses, physiotherapists etc. and the problems tackled can be viewed holistically, in terms of the whole treatment for a patient, rather than seeing the roles of the individual specialists in isolation. In engineering, mechanical engineers may be asked to work with electrical and civil engineers to complete 'real world' projects in small groups.

There is no doubt that each discipline inherently has its own language, culture and ways of doing things (Becher 1989) and in order to learn how to work effectively across the disciplinary divides, students need opportunities to work together, otherwise they will find themselves disadvantaged when they do join mixed work teams in the future.

ISSUES OF MONITORING AND MANAGING SUPPORT

For students it is difficult to hide and go unseen in a SGT session. So for the tutor it becomes an opportunity to informally monitor progress and to spot any difficulties before they become major problems. Many tutors are asked to keep a simple register of attendance as it has long been known that those who don't turn up are much more likely to fail the module or course. The reasons why students don't come to class are as varied as the students themselves and in practice the SGT tutor is more likely than most to have insight into what lies behind the absence. Tutorials can sometimes be considered as providing a pastoral role in addition to the academic focus already discussed. In such circumstances the tutor seeks to develop an ongoing relationship with their students that may span their entire time at university or college. The tutor often performs certain administrative functions, such as communicating exam results and feedback to their personal tutees. The tutor may also be involved in supporting the use of personal development profiles (PDPs) which are student-owned portfolios used to record and evidence a student's academic, personal and professional development. Many departments use their tutorial system to support the student in understanding and using their PDP.

In a SGT session it is possible to detect and respond to individual differences and needs. A student may have a particular disability, the most commonly occurring being dyslexia and sight and hearing difficulties. The Special Educational Needs and Disability Act (SENDA) 2001 gives clear responsibility to teachers and universities to take positive and anticipatory steps so that they do not discriminate against students with disabilities. Within a small group context the teacher can work with their students and, on an individual basis, tactfully discover what 'reasonable adjustments' can be made in teaching, learning and assessment activities to ensure equity and inclusivity in the classroom (see Chapter 10 for further information).

Tutors can find themselves in the role of counsellor or adviser in small group sessions. As the students and tutor have established a level of rapport and trust, it is not uncommon for the SGT tutor to be the student's first port of call if a problem occurs. The tutor may be able to offer advice on academic matters, listen to personal problems and provide a referral to those in the institution with expertise to help further. So through SGT, personal and professional relationships can develop which provide ongoing support for our students. It is very likely that much of the key face-to-face contact between teachers and students happens in SGT sessions and this is a vital ingredient for study in most universities and colleges.

EXAMPLES FROM DIFFERENT DISCIPLINES

Teachers were asked to briefly summarize their views on 'What are the goals of SGT in your discipline?' and to try to capture what SGT is intended to achieve in their disciplines.

History

- Using in-depth exploration of a topic.
- Learning how to make an academic argument.
- Appreciating that there is rarely a 'right and wrong' but that it is about interpreting evidence.

Physics

- Seeing that there is more than one way of solving a problem.
- Providing students with individual feedback and help.
- Giving the students encouragement to practise – you have to learn by doing in physics.

Medicine

- We need students to think for themselves, not to digest the textbook.
- It is important that our students know how to find out things for themselves and can update their knowledge.
- Communication skills are also very important.

Law

- The students need to prepare for class; they need to have done the readings to be able to discuss them sensibly and knowledgeably.
- Students should debate, discuss and learn how to put their points across.
- Students can also ask questions if they don't understand or want further information.

FURTHER READING AND A USEFUL WEB SITE

To find out more about the theories and models to explain *How Students Learn* please refer to the online guide that supports this book series, specially prepared for busy new teachers by George Brown (2004). The URL is www.routledgefalmer.com/series/KGETHE

Chapter 2

Conditions for successful SGT

INTRODUCTION

As discussed in Chapter 1, achieving the goals of SGT has such enormous educational benefits that it is essential that every effort is made to ensure that the correct conditions for achieving them are met. Clearly the skills of the facilitator are of major importance but these will be left for Chapter 3, where they can be examined in more detail. Here we will concentrate on describing the practical, organizational and interpersonal conditions that will allow the group to reach its optimal potential. If these conditions can be met, an effective small group will be produced that will achieve deep learning.

PREPARATION

In teaching, preparation is everything. Many of the problems that arise in SGT can be prevented by good preparation and foresight. Knowing your group and knowing your curriculum may seem obvious, but from an analysis of student feedback reports, it is surprising the number of teachers who turn up to SGT sessions and ask the students 'Who are you and what are we supposed to be doing?'

Know your curriculum

Teachers in HE should be fully aware of the overall curriculum their students are following, an issue that should be resolved by good course co-ordination. With modularization students can take a variety of paths through a degree course and hence have a variety of learning experiences. Even within a module or course, communication between multiple teachers may often be problematic. Hence it is important that the SGT facilitator knows where the session they are leading fits into the big curriculum picture.

Know your group

As will be discussed later in more detail, the importance of the relationships that develop between teachers and students and between students is of fundamental importance to the success of SGT. Therefore it is essential that the SGT facilitator makes an effort to find out who their students are, particularly on the first occasion they meet. For example it is useful to have a list of the students' names, to know what courses they are on and what year they are. Having this information beforehand ensures that an idea can be obtained of their background knowledge and experience. Clearly more detailed knowledge can be obtained once the group starts and develops, but letting students know that you know who they are right from the beginning will greatly facilitate subsequent interpersonal relationships and interactions.

Structure learning

All learning episodes need to be structured for effectiveness and even the more open-ended nature of SGT requires good organization. The conventional sequence is a beginning, where the context for the learning is established, a middle where the content is dealt with and an end where closure takes place. In SGT the context includes introductions, warm-up and ice-breaking, and the establishment of ground rules and learning outcomes. The content includes all the SGT activities and closure involves reaching conclusions and summarizing.

Having aims and outcomes

In a constructively aligned HE curriculum (Biggs 1999) with a well-defined programme specification, all learning experiences such as lectures, seminars, practical sessions, self-directed learning and small group teaching sessions should fit together into a coherent and integrated whole. They should be embedded in a matrix of learning outcomes (see Brown 2004). If different teaching methods are more effective at achieving the acquisition of specific learning outcomes then what sort of learning outcomes are appropriate for SGT? SGT is so flexible that it can in principle be used to achieve learning outcomes right across the whole of the domains of learning. As discussed in Chapter 1, the broad goals of SGT are the development of deep-level understanding, interpersonal and practical skills and attitudinal change; clearly outcomes in these areas are more suitable for SGT. Although factual knowledge may be acquired during SGT sessions, this should not be the primary focus of the session. On the other hand applying, using and elaborating factual knowledge is ideally suited to SGT.

The facilitator should therefore have a broad idea of what learning outcomes might be suitable for the SGT session before it starts. These may be more or less well defined or they may be outcomes that develop as the session progresses. In addition, as discussed shortly, outcomes may be generated by the group and in certain cases this might actually be the focus of the session.

Resources

While many SGT sessions can function without any resources other than the participants' own knowledge and skills, some sessions might require specific resources to enhance the learning experience and these must be prepared beforehand. There are such a wide variety of SGT sessions that the types of resources potentially required are endless: books, worksheets, handouts, envelopes, cards, pens, acetate transparencies, *Blu Tac*, drawing pins, flip charts and so on.

Resources such as reference books can be used to ensure that factual material under discussion is up-to-date and accurate. In most cases there is little point in allowing challenging discussions to take place if key facts are not established and agreed on. (In the case of PBL this 'rule' can be broken as the aim of the first session is to establish a set of learning outcomes: see Chapter 5.)

If the SGT session is being used to introduce and practise practical skills then clearly appropriate sets of equipment must be available for students.

GETTING THE CONDITIONS RIGHT: MASLOW'S HIERARCHY

The goals of SGT are optimized if participants are physically, rationally and emotionally comfortable and are spatially and temporally organized in appropriate ways. A useful framework for thinking about these

15

TABLE 2.1 Maslow's hierarchy of needs

Hierarchy of needs	Implications for facilitators and SGT
Self-actualization needs	Encourage personal growth with enthusiasm, support, encouragement, positivity and optimism.
Self-esteem needs: pride, achievement, mastery	Encourage independence, praise performance, welcome new ideas, treat students with dignity. Be optimistic and supportive.
Social needs: acceptance, love, belonging	Facilitator should have a caring attitude towards participants. Groups should be encouraged to interact and bond by means of appropriate warm-up activities and collaborative tasks.
Safety and shelter needs: safe from harm, security, stability, order and structure	Treat participants with respect and honesty. Ensure participants remain within a psychological comfort zone with minimum anxiety, respecting personal privacy and confidentiality. Treat students fairly, maintain accurate information, abide by safety rules.
Physical and physiological needs: food, shelter and comfort	Make sure rooms are big enough, well ventilated and temperature controlled. Ensure seats are comfortable. Participants need regular breaks for food, drink and the toilet.

conditions is Maslow's hierarchy of needs, which essentially applies to all forms of education and human relationships, but is particularly helpful when trying to understand the conditions necessary for effective SGT (Maslow 1968). See Table 2.1.

The implication of Maslow's hierarchy is that needs at any particular level cannot be dealt with adequately unless needs at the level below have been fulfilled.

Physical conditions

Group size

If one of the goals of SGT is to get people to talk, clearly the number of potential conversationalists involved will influence the degree to which this can be achieved for any particular individual. Two people can clearly have a fairly equitable discussion but what they talk about will be limited to their own knowledge and experience. Increasing the numbers involved will inject greater variety into the debate and may expose individuals to a variety of alternative viewpoints that they had not previously considered. But if group numbers are increased above a certain level, individual contributions will be minimized and some people may find themselves inhibited from talking for reasons that will be discussed later. Therefore there must be a small group size that optimizes both the variety of knowledge, experience and viewpoints available and the opportunity for individual oral contributions. Evidence suggests this number is roughly from five to eight people, although with appropriate facilitation, and with an experienced group, it can be extended upwards (Jaques 2000). SGT can be part of a larger teaching environment so that large groups can be broken up into small groups and back again during, for example, a workshop.

Group arrangements

The physical arrangement of participants will also influence how they interact and hence achieve the aims of the SGT session. Participants may be allowed to enter the room and sit where they like. However, unless they are experienced in SGT, it is unlikely they will arrange themselves in the best configuration. Of course once seated they can be rearranged by appropriate and sensitive facilitation, but it is best to avoid this by organizing the seating in the room beforehand.

The way the seats are arranged in teaching sessions sends a powerful message to learners. The traditional lecture theatre or seminar room has the teacher at the front of rows of parallel seats and all teachers are familiar with the student dynamics leading from this arrangement. Students tend to fill up the rows from the back (to avoid teacher interaction or surveillance?) with the front seats deliberately occupied by the keenest students, or reluctantly by late-comers. This frontal and linear arrangement sends the message that teaching and learning is a 'transmission' process. In SGT the number of rows is potentially much smaller but the same dynamic can apply. Since, according to the goals of small group teaching, non-participation is not an option, allowing students to sit at the back to avoid interacting with the group or the teacher becomes something the facilitator must avoid. Hence the best arrangement that prevents this situation happening right from the start is a circular or semicircular arrangement of seats (Jaques 2000; Quinn 2000; Elwyn *et al.* 2001). This has the added advantage of ensuring that all participants can see and maintain eye contact with each other and the facilitator. (If SGT is taking place in a larger room with fixed seats, then alternative arrangements can be made, e.g. two rows of four facing each other, to achieve roughly the same aim.) In addition it is best if the facilitator is present when students arrive so that they can be shepherded into their seats and inhibited from rearranging the furniture. In larger groups putting out the chairs so that students sit in mini-groupings can help syndicate work.

Facilitator position

In a circular or semicircular arrangement of students, where should the facilitator sit? We will say more about the skills and attitudes of the facilitator in Chapter 3 but just like the configuration of the group, the position of the facilitator with respect to the group sends important educational messages. If the facilitator stands up at the front or adopts a mainly frontal position, the proceedings may be dominated by the facilitator's presence and the SGT session may descend into transmission mode. On the other hand if the facilitator sits with the group, as part of the circle, occasionally getting up to use a flip chart or blackboard, or even getting one of the students to do any writing, then the facilitator is more likely to generate the type of group dynamics that will encourage discussion and interpersonal interactions between group members. So whenever possible, join the circle.

Room size

Clearly the room should be large enough for a small group to fit in with space for books, writing surfaces, flip charts and the use of any other equipment that is necessary. If a choice is available, small rooms are more suitable for small groups but sometimes it is necessary for multiple SGT sessions to take place in a larger room or even a raked lecture theatre. The advantage of a circular grouping becomes apparent in such situations since group members form an inward facing coherent unit that can concentrate on their task without too much outside interference. In this way sometimes hundreds of students can be split into tens of small groups that can quite readily achieve most of the aims of SGT with appropriate facilitation and organization.

Interpersonal conditions

Unlike lecturing, where students are largely passive and there is usually limited interaction between students and the lecturer, SGT thrives on talking, debate, discussion and argument. However, students need to feel comfortable engaging in these activities; if they don't feel the conditions are right, they will be inhibited from participation and may even be actively hostile. This is where the facilitator's interpersonal skills are most important and where they must work hard to set up the right *context* for the SGT session. First impressions are everything and if the facilitator can begin the SGT session in the right way, many of the potential problems of SGT can be avoided. On the other hand if little effort is made to ensure the interpersonal conditions are correct, then the group might begin to dysfunction right from the start. In this section we take a look at a range of activities that need to be carried out early on in a SGT session that will create the right conditions and context for deep learning. Clearly the extent to which these need to be engaged in depends on the how familiar the group is with itself and with the facilitator. In the case of a new group, they are more or less mandatory but more experienced groups could dispense with some of them.

Warming-up, introductions and ice-breaking

When groups of humans get together for the first time, depending on the cultural context, there is a period of insecurity and anxiety during which they attempt consciously or subconsciously to work out who people are, who's in charge, who's threatening, friendly, attractive, etc. Depending on the levels of people's self-confidence, introversion or extraversion, individuals may talk openly, ask questions, listen and respond to what people are saying or merely observe other people's behaviour and body language. With groups of students who know each other, this process may be minimized but with new groups of students or heterogeneous multi-professional groups it will be a significant feature of their first moments together.

One of the key aims of SGT is to encourage people to talk to each other and to ensure that everyone contributes. The good facilitator should begin by reducing anxiety and optimizing the self-confidence of the group, hence ensuring good interpersonal relations later on. So for example once students are settled down in their seats it might be useful to say:

> Welcome to today's session on X, Y and Z. Before we get into the main part of our time together, as we are a new group, I think it would be nice if we spent just a few minutes introducing ourselves. I hope that by doing this you will feel a little less anxious about what's going to happen.

Some people will actually find this even more anxiety provoking: you are being asked to speak in front of a group of unknown peers, in public. That is why it's useful for the facilitator to provide some boundaries and a framework for this activity. Putting a time limit ('just a few minutes') on the proceedings clearly shows that detailed biographies are not being asked for. Most people in a small group don't mind saying their name, what course they're on or where they're from. However, to make it less stressful, you can ask students to introduce themselves to each other. Getting them to talk to each other acts as a warm-up or ice-breaking activity (see Chapter 4 for specific methods of doing this). Of course the facilitators should also engage in this process as well, maybe sitting down and talking to a student without a partner or introducing themselves to a group of two. Getting students to wear name badges is a good idea so that group members can get to know each other's names. From this point on, a variety of more elaborate warm-up or ice-breaking activities can take place depending on the facilitator's aims and the degree to which the group needs to be made more coherent.

The process of encouraging group introductions and maybe participating in a more elaborate ice-breaking activity should reduce initial anxiety levels and make group members feel more comfortable with each other. There may still be some group members who still feel that it was all a waste of time and 'why don't you get on with it'. We will come to them later.

Ground rules: transferable skill outcomes

Before moving into the substantive part of the SGT session it is useful to establish some ground rules with the group. This is particularly important with a new group or with a group that you will be facilitating over a period of weeks or months. Ground rules form an attitudinal and rational framework for all subsequent work with the group. The facilitator can in principle impose a pre-existing set of ground rules on the group but a more democratic approach, which will gain more respect from the group, is to get students to come up with a set of ground rules themselves. For this they will probably require guidance; the facilitator's knowledge of ground rules that other groups have used before will be very useful.

However, like everything else in SGT, the very idea of ground rules needs to be broached sensitively. It is best introduced in the context of the overall aims and outcomes for SGT. Before detailing the aims and outcomes of the specific session, or if necessary negotiating them with the group as described later, it is useful to mention the transferable skill outcomes that are a major feature of all SGT (see Chapter 1). Table 1.2 outlines what they are; it is useful to bring them to the attention of the group and to stress that in parallel with the acquisition of specific outcomes from each session, students will also acquire a set of interpersonal communication skill outcomes that are just as important. If the students understand this then they might be encouraged to think what type of ground rules they produce might achieve them.

Here is a list of suggestions for ground rules, some of which might be chosen as a framework for SGT:

- All students as far as possible should contribute their ideas and opinions to the discussion.
- Respect other people's point of view.
- Don't interrupt anyone when they're speaking.
- Don't dominate the discussion, give others a chance to speak.
- Criticize people's arguments, not their personality.
- Listen to what other people are saying.
- There are no 'stupid' questions.
- Keep group discussions confidential outside the group.
- Keep to the aims and outcomes of the session.
- Try to remain focused on the specified tasks.
- Members should feel responsibility towards achieving group aims.
- Perform required preparation tasks outside the group.
- Group members accept the ground rules.

Aims and outcomes

The fundamental importance of clear aims and outcomes in developing and implementing a constructively aligned curriculum has been mentioned earlier. As discussed in Chapter 1, one of the key aims of SGT is 'deep learning', meaning that students should be able to apply, practise and elaborate their knowledge. SGT provides opportunities for students to analyse the assumptions they have about their knowledge, to ask challenging questions and to critically evaluate the meanings they are trying to construct. Thus most of the aims and outcomes that inform SGT are at the higher end of the cognitive and attitudinal domain. Some forms of SGT will also deal with the acquisition of psychomotor or practical skills (see Chapter 7).

Unless aims and outcomes are to be negotiated, as we shall discuss, the facilitator should have a clear idea of what they are and how they fit with the overall specification of the course. If they have not already been published in course documentation they should communicate them to the students at an appropriate point at the beginning of the session. The acceptance of these aims and outcomes by the group will then focus the SGT session.

Activation of prior learning

However, aims and outcomes should not just be plucked out of the air and placed before the group. They should gradually be introduced as the context of the session is introduced and revealed. Although the overall title of the session may have been mentioned earlier, and hence students will know roughly what area it is concerned with, it might be useful to begin by briefly going over some previous work and asking a few simple questions to establish what prior knowledge they have. (Questioning skills will be further dealt with in Chapter 3 but briefly, the use of fairly easy closed questions, checking on previous knowledge at the beginning of a session, will encourage students to attempt to answer. More complex open-ended questions should be saved until later.) Building on this 'activation of prior learning' a more detailed introduction of the content of the SGT session might then be made, pointing out how relevant and important it is for students to have an opportunity to deal with this information. Finally the specific aims and outcomes can be outlined and explained.

Sometimes it is appropriate for students to generate their own learning outcomes. This is a fundamental feature of PBL (discussed in Chapter 5), but it may occur in more conventional forms of SGT. In fact it is often useful to discuss with students if they have any specific outcomes that they might like to achieve from a SGT session. (The ground rules might even specify that students can contribute learning outcomes.) In some cases student-generated learning outcomes might not align with the overall curriculum requirements but in other cases the facilitator might agree that they are a useful contribution and might make provision to deal with them. Sometimes further learning outcomes emerge during the session and the facilitator should be responsive enough to incorporate them.

Task explanations

Introductions have been made, the context of the session has been outlined and the aims and outcomes have been made clear to the students. Next come the various activities, ranging from a simple guided discussion to a complete workshop, that make up the many activities found in SGT (see Chapter 4). At this point it is useful to outline the structure and organization of the rest of the session, 'signposting' the various activities that will be undertaken, the approximate time they will take and any other relevant items of information about the session. After this point the focus of the group changes radically and needs to be managed effectively by the facilitator. The emphasis must be on clear and unambiguous instructions that all group members understand, as it is often at this point that problems first arise. If members have been given individual or group tasks to perform it is essential that they know precisely what they are supposed to do, how long they should take, what they should do when they have finished and what they should do if they need help. It is surprising how many people don't pay attention when being given instructions and then expect other group members to tell them what to do. Depending on the complexity and variety of the tasks and the number of groups involved, clear oral explanations may be all that is needed but putting them on a flip chart or providing a handout will often prevent confusion.

KEEPING ON TRACK: MONITORING PROGRESS

Once the group has been set up and is working, the facilitator needs to keep an eye on the group ensuring that they are remaining on task, and moving towards achieving their aims and outcomes. The facilitator may be actively involved by, for example, running a small group discussion in which they are a participant or they may have given the rest of the group or groups specific tasks to perform and be merely observing. In all cases they need to monitor and record progress, keep an eye on group dynamics and be aware of the overall structure of the session and its time management. The facilitator needs specific skills to deal with these (see Chapter 3). Here some overall suggestions on maintaining effective conditions for a SGT to function are described.

Timing and time management

Effective time management is of crucial importance in SGT because its more open-ended structure makes time management potentially more difficult. For example discussions might go on longer than anticipated and facilitators might be reluctant to stop participants talking when an interesting and relevant point is being made or unexpected questions might arise which need answering. Nevertheless keeping to overall time boundaries and ensuring that discussions, questions and activities are kept within specific time limits not only ensures that the session is well organized but also makes certain that the aims and outcomes of the session will be met. Good time management and organization also instils confidence in the participants, which translates into good group dynamics. There is nothing more boring to a student than to be involved in a rambling SGT session where the time to complete tasks is either too long or too short, where the boundaries between different activities are blurred and indistinct, and where the amount of time for the whole session is ill defined or even absent.

Questioning

Although different types of questions and the facilitator's questioning skills will be discussed in more detail in Chapter 3, the use of questions is essential to monitor the group's progress. As described earlier the use of questions at the beginning of the session establishes and activates prior learning and the types of questions used can have a significant influence on group dynamics. However, later in the session questions can be used to see if participants have completed specific tasks or are discussing issues at an appropriate level and reaching towards the required learning outcomes. If the aim of SGT is deep learning, the questions that are aimed at participants during this phase should encourage deep level thinking. Questions focused on analysis, application, critical evaluation and problem solving, for example, become crucial. Finally, during closure at the end of the session, questions can be used to see if the group have completed their tasks and have achieved their learning outcomes.

Recording achievements and progress

In some cases it is necessary to record the progress and the products of the group during a SGT session. For example during a 'brainstorming' activity, ideas need to be written down for subsequent analysis and prioritizing; during a discussion, opinions and questions might need to be recorded. During closure it might be useful to write down the conclusions of the group. This recording can be performed by students in notebooks or handouts or by the facilitator on a flip chart or over-head transparency.

DEALING WITH TYPES OF GROUPS AND GROUP DYNAMICS

The perfect group knows exactly what it is supposed to be doing and works collaboratively towards achieving its agreed deep learning goals. They have been warmed up by the facilitator, who has made sure the group members have introduced themselves, they have decided on ground rules, they are aware of the context and the goals of the session, and they feel comfortable with and have a clear understanding of the activities they are to engage in. Group members engage in deep-level discussions or carry out challenging tasks and activities that push them to the edge of their knowledge and experience. The facilitator keeps them on track by monitoring progress and the use of judicious questioning and expert time management. Finally, closure is achieved with all outcomes summarized and met. This ideal situation is difficult to achieve in practice but is one that should be aimed for by all good SGT facilitators.

However, there are many different types of small groups and innumerable types of actions and interactions occurring within them. The following sections will look at how the ideas discussed above on the conditions necessary to create an effective group can be applied in different circumstances and will also look at the ways in which groups can become dysfunctional, suggesting methods for dealing with them.

The 'one-off' group

In the one-off group, where students do not necessarily know each other or the facilitator beforehand and where they may not meet again, the key issue becomes warming the participants up and encouraging them to talk to each other. Therefore a special emphasis should be placed on anxiety-reducing measures: friendly introductions, ice-breaking activities, non-threatening questioning to activate prior learning and clear unambiguous instructions and goals. Because the group may not be seen again for further sessions, it may be worthwhile minimizing the amount of time spent on producing ground rules and possibly recommending a commonly agreed set. After slightly more time spent on introductions and contextualization, the rest of the session can proceed normally.

The 'regular' group

Considerable learning benefits can be obtained with a regular group that meets, for example, once a week over a term or semester. The main advantage is that group members get to know each other, leading to better group interactivity and improved collaboration. This enables more complex issues to be dealt with and more and varied activities to be engaged in. After introductions, ice-breaking and ground rules have been established in the first meeting, these activities can be minimized in subsequent sessions and hence more time can be spent on dealing with the content. Regular meetings mean that it is possible to give participants tasks or presentations to prepare for each session; it is an ideal environment for student-led seminars (as will be discussed later in Chapter 6). Rotating specific responsibilities around the group week by week also gives participants opportunities to try out and develop useful skills such as group leadership, recording and summarizing progress, chairing discussions, making short presentations or demonstrating practical procedures.

Seeing group members over an extended period of time also enables the observant facilitator to monitor the growth and development of their interpersonal skills, the depth of their thinking, their strengths and weaknesses in particular situations and the maturing of their attitudes. Sensitive individual feedback from the facilitator can enhance all these developments.

Potential disadvantages of regular small groups are that some group members may develop antipathy towards each other which might inhibit collaboration or even cause outright conflict. However, as will be discussed later, a good facilitator will watch out for the development of such problems and hopefully prevent them happening or minimize their effect on group dynamics.

Sometimes the membership of a regular group changes either due to illness or other absence and new group members may appear. It is important that new members are fully integrated into the group as soon as possible to maintain cohesion. A special attempt should be made to ensure that new members are introduced effectively and are allowed to 'bond' with existing group members. Allowing them to pair up on a rotating basis with other group members is a useful way of letting them get to know other each other.

The mixed group

Rather than having group members from the same course in the same year, a mixed group might consist of members who differ in some significant way from each other. For example students from different courses (e.g. medics and nurses) or different years of the same course or even staff, students and administrators. Modularization in HE has led to students with varied backgrounds and degree aims ending up studying the same modules, so the occurrence of mixed groups is not uncommon. Again helping such a group to function effectively involves laying emphasis on getting the group introduced, warmed up and contexualized. However, with a mixed group the most important issue is to openly *acknowledge differences* right from the start and stress the advantages that will develop from this. Thus, if facilitators are aware of the differences in background, knowledge and experience of group members (and this should be discovered anyway during the introductions phase) they can positively build on this in the various discussions and tasks that the group might engage in. Encouraging students to explore their different knowledge bases together can lead to much useful learning, via peer teaching and the sharing of experiences. Diversity in SGT is dealt with in more detail in Chapter 10.

THE PROBLEM OR DYSFUNCTIONAL GROUP

Small groups can become dysfunctional for a variety of reasons, either from poor facilitation and organization or by the actions of individual group members. In all cases prevention is better than cure; the best way for a facilitator to deal with the problem of a dysfunctional group is not to let it become dysfunctional in the first place by paying attention to preparation, outcomes, warm-up and the monitoring of group dynamics and progress. Some examples of dysfunctional groups and some suggestions on how to avoid them are now discussed.

Dysfunctional organization

Groups can become dysfunctional if the facilitator does not pay attention to setting up, organization and monitoring. The members of a group that have not been 'formed' correctly, because of inadequate introductions or ice-breaking, might feel anxious and apprehensive. Members could then be reluctant to talk or participate in activities; in addition they might feel hostile towards a facilitator who has pitched them into an uncomfortable situation. Giving the group ill-defined, inappropriate, irrelevant or unachievable tasks will also cause problems. Activities should be appropriate to the level of the group, should be clearly explained and should be capable of completion during the session. The facilitator should check beforehand that activities are not too complex to be feasibly completed within the time available, or alternatively that they are not too trivial to be completed with excessive and unplanned time to spare. The skills of the facilitator are the most important element in creating an effective group (these will be outlined further in Chapter 3). However, even with good facilitation, problems can still arise within groups as discussed in the following sections.

Dealing with group conflict

In many ways conflict is an essential feature of many SGT sessions, although different people will have different views on what conflict means in this context. Much of SGT is about encouraging people to expose their views and opinions to others and to engage in debate and argument. This will inevitably lead some group members to challenge the assumptions and beliefs of others, which can be a painful experience leading to outright conflict and even hostility. However, this can often be precisely the level of debate required since one of the goals of SGT must be to encourage participants to go below the surface and examine the reasons why they believe what they do. 'Cognitive dissonance' is the term used to describe the state in which someone is confronted by a perception, an idea or a fact that does not fit into their cognitive framework (Festinger 1957). It can be painful and anxiety provoking but at the same time it is one of the most powerful learning experiences there is, enabling the student, once the conflict has been resolved, to construct even deeper understanding (Kolb 1984). If the facilitator makes it clear during the introductory phase that disagreement and conflict might arise, but that participants should work through it as it will lead to a deeper understanding, then a positive outcome can be achieved. Emphasizing ground rules that remind participants that it is better to attack people's arguments, not their personalities, can further ensure that hostilities are avoided.

The facilitator needs to monitor the degree to which conflict has been raised; individual facilitators will have different thresholds for dealing with this. The facilitator needs to be aware of how the conflict has been caused: is it a difference of perception, opinion, fact or belief, is it serious or trivial? Can the presentation of information help to resolve it? Can the facilitator rephrase the conflicting problem so that participants can see how it is caused by, for example, assumptions that they were not aware of? Is it due to different personality types or learning styles? By sensitively monitoring SGT debates, facilitators should be able to prevent 'normal' argument and debate turning into open hostility and a breakdown of collaborative learning.

Dealing with dominant group members

One of the commonest questions asked by novice facilitators is 'How can I deal with one member of the group who dominates the discussion and prevents others from fully participating?' As mentioned earlier, the best approach is to try to avoid this situation in the first place through adequate introductions, warm-up and ground-rule acceptance. Nevertheless despite a facilitator's best endeavours, it will still arise and strategies need to be adopted to deal with it. Reminding the group of the ground rules on participation might work, plus a gentle comment: 'John, you've made quite a lot of interesting points, can we hear from someone else?' or 'John, thank you for your contribution so far, but I think it's important that everyone has a say, so can you just put yourself on hold for a while please and let's see what Jane thinks about this issue.' Using names can be very useful in this situation as you can specifically ask individuals to come in and join the debate. An alternative strategy is to go round the group in turn asking each participant to make a contribution. Breaking the group up into smaller groupings or

29

pairs to allow individuals to talk to each other will also prevent domination by one individual and allow other individuals the opportunity to discuss. Depending on the circumstances a quiet word in the ear at an appropriate moment in a group activity might suffice. If you have identified more than one dominant member, try putting them all in the same subgroup; at least one of them will have to learn how to keep quiet!

If dominant behaviour still continues and threatens to disrupt the goals of the group, then stronger methods are called for. The facilitator should try to convince the group to agree that it finds the contribution of the individual excessive and that they should remain quiet for a while. This use of peer pressure can often be more effective than requests from the facilitator. Beyond this the facilitator has the responsibility of the 'greatest good of the greatest number' and might be forced to ask the problem participant to leave the group. However, this should be followed up by arranging to counsel the 'offender' to explain the importance of group collaboration and sticking to ground rules to achieve group outcomes.

Dealing with passive group members

Another common problem encountered by facilitators is the very quiet group whose members are reluctant to participate. Here the most important thing to do is to warm the group up and perform ice-breakers that will get members feeling comfortable with each other. However, the problem might also be caused by a boring, trivial or overwhelmingly complex aim, so it is important to ensure that the activity the group are engaging in is relevant and important, and that the group are aware of this.

Dealing with a non-participating individual

It might take a while for a facilitator to spot non-participation but he or she should be watching out for it right from the start. Since one of the goals of SGT is the development of interpersonal communication skills, non-participation is not an option and should be made clear to participants when discussing ground rules. At the beginning of a session and at any time during it, merely getting group members to talk in pairs about an issue can act as a catalyst for further open discussion. However, a non-participating individual might be very shy, might be filled with anxiety or might be feeling ill. It is the facilitator's role to attempt to sensitively diagnose the situation while keeping the group going at the same time. Simply asking the individual by name: 'James, what's your view on this?' followed by some more clarification questions to bring him or her more into the discussion might work.

Dealing with cynical group members

Some participants, particularly those with a strong predilection for passive learning, find SGT a problem. They see SGT with its 'touchy-feely' and discussion orientated emphasis as a waste of time. They are dominated by the idea of content and surface learning and they want to be told the answers. What they lack is an understanding of the importance of *process* in learning, of the interpersonal and teamwork skills they will develop as a result of talking, collaborating and asking questions and the possibility of deep learning.

Dealing with this issue, which can cause disruption to SGT sessions, is really a problem of orientating students towards metacognition and developing appropriate ways of learning; it could be part of an induction programme for new students. On the other hand facilitators should be able to emphasize the importance of engaging in process during the introductory phase of SGT sessions. Rewarding 'cynical' participants with positive feedback on their contributions and specifically trying to emphasize the importance of their knowledge to the rest of the group can also help to bring down the barriers these students might have when dealing with SGT episodes.

FURTHER READING

Elwyn, G., Greenhalgh, T. and Macfarlane, F. (2001) *Groups: A Guide to Small Group Work in Healthcare, Management, Education and Research*, London: Radcliffe Medical Press.

Jaques, D. (2000) *Learning in Groups: A Handbook for Improving Group Work*, 3rd edn, London: Kogan Page.

Westberg, J. and Jason, H. (1996) *Fostering Learning in Small Groups: A Practical Guide*, New York: Springer.

Chapter 3

The skills of facilitation

ATTITUDES TOWARDS TEACHING AND LEARNING

In this chapter we will examine the crucial role that facilitators play in SGT, particularly the attitudes towards teaching and learning that they should have, and the interpersonal and questioning skills they need if they are to run effective small groups.

If one of the fundamental goals of SGT is to encourage participants to talk, to debate, to question and to engage in deep learning activities, then facilitators must adopt a particular standpoint with respect to their own attitude to teaching and learning which encourages these processes. For example, the conventional view of the teacher is of a person who transmits information, who makes presentations and lectures, and who controls and organizes largely passive learners.

However, modern educational frameworks have moved away from this 'teacher-centred' approach towards a more 'learner-centred' model where the learner's needs and his or her existing knowledge and skills are built on in an active, collaborative and democratic way. In this framework the teacher becomes a facilitator of learning, recognizing the autonomy of individuals and the responsibility they have towards their own personal growth and development. It is this attitude that the successful SGT facilitator must have.

For some teachers, abandoning their 'transmitter' role and adopting a more learner-centred approach can be quite difficult. It can mean giving up providing information, no longer telling students facts, no longer being at the centre of knowledge and the personal power that comes with it.

> To reject didactic teaching, is to reject teaching itself.
>
> (Chris Woodhead)

For other teachers, it is a liberation and an acknowledgement of something they have always known: that students learn best when they are in control and take responsibility for their own learning.

> As I began to trust students . . . I changed from being a teacher . . . to being a facilitator of learning.
>
> (Carl Rogers 1983: 26)

Because there are many different types of SGT, ranging from student-led seminars to free-flowing discussions to problem based learning, facilitators can adopt a variety of positions with respect to the nature of the learning taking place and their role in helping its acquisition. There is a spectrum of intervention, from total control at one end to complete hands-off approach at the other. For successful SGT facilitation, the facilitators must be able to position themselves at an appropriate point on this spectrum compatible with the membership of the group and the overall aims of the session. In addition they must be flexible enough to move along this spectrum depending on the evolving aims and dynamics of particular groups.

MODELS OF TEACHING, LEARNING AND FACILITATION

There are a number of educational frameworks that can be used to help facilitators develop appropriate attitudes towards their role. These frameworks also apply to education as a whole, human relations, counselling, appraisal and a wide variety of other interpersonal situations, but they are particularly suited to SGT. There are two relevant types. First, theories of self-actualization and student-centredness, which are essentially concerned with the nature of learners and the empathy and respect that facilitators should demonstrate towards them. Second, theories of group dynamics, which help facilitators deal with the overall actions of the group and interpersonal interactions between its members.

The nature of learners

A fundamental issue in that branch of philosophy called epistemology concerns the status of human knowledge. How do we acquire 'true' knowledge? Are we born with innate knowledge and a 'human nature'? Or is each of us born into the world as a blank slate or tabula rasa on which experience writes. How flexible and plastic are our minds? Is nature or nurture more important in what we become? This debate has been reviewed by Pinker (2002), who challenges the 'blank slate' approach and asserts the primacy of a complex human nature. From an educational perspective the answers we give to these questions have profound effects on how we structure our educational institutions and more importantly how as teachers and facilitators, we interact with our learners. For example, if we think learners are blank slates, we may feel that we can mould and manipulate them as we please and implant any knowledge as we see fit.

> Give me a child for the first seven years and I'll show you the man.
>
> (Jesuit saying)

On the other hand, if learners have a 'nature' and if cognition has functional elements that have evolved over millions of years, then facilitators need to be aware of and work with the grain of human nature to achieve optimal effectiveness.

Self-actualization

Abraham Maslow (1954) argued that an important motivating factor in human behaviour is 'the need to become as much as one can possibly become': to *self-actualize*. As outlined earlier, each person has a hierarchy of needs that must be satisfied, ranging from basic physiological requirements to love, esteem and, finally, self-actualization itself. For facilitators this should lead to a basic awareness that physical comfort and anxiety reduction leads towards effective SGT (see Table 2.1, p. 16).

Carl Rogers, who also supported the concept of self-actualization, developed his individually orientated psychotherapeutic ideas to deal with the optimum type of human relationships that would lead to educational effectiveness. His book, *Freedom to Learn for the 80s* (Rogers 1983), had a profound influence on adult educational practice.

Roger's key principles are that individuals have a self-actualizing tendency towards the achievement of their own potential, they have a unique self-concept, need positive self-regard, and should be trusted to self-actualize. The implications for teachers and facilitators are that students need their individuality respected and require those with whom they interact to demonstrate a positive and trusting attitude, personal genuiness and empathy. Thus Rogers emphasized that teaching and facilitation is above all else a *human relationship*.

Further implications are that facilitators should engender a climate of trust in which curiosity and the intrinsic desire to learn can be nourished and enhanced. Students should be allowed to participate in decisions about their learning. Facilitators should help students build their confidence and self-esteem and encourage them to take responsibility for their own learning, so becoming lifelong learners. All of these ideas can be seen as important attributes and attitudes that facilitators need if they are to run successful small groups.

Student-centred learning

This important educational concept, which underpins much modern educational practice, can be traced back to a number of thinkers in the eighteenth and nineteenth centuries such as Rousseau (1762) and Froebel (1886). However, it was articulated most clearly by the American philosopher John Dewey (1916) who asserted that the educational process must start with and build upon the interests of the learner; that it must involve both thinking and activity, that the teacher should be a guide and co-worker rather than someone who prescribes rigid learning tasks and that the goal of education should be the growth of the individual. Again these ideas strongly resonate with the concept of self-actualization described earlier and can be seen as leading towards particular modes of facilitation in SGT.

Student-centredness is also underpinned by ideas from modern psychology which emphasize the importance of the learner's own cognitive framework as a platform for building further knowledge and understanding. The famous quotation by Ausubel, 'The most important factor influencing learning is what the learner already knows, ascertain this and teach accordingly' (Ausubel 1968), can be seen as the underlying principle of the constructivist view of learning. The common exhortation, aimed at trainee school teachers, that they should 'start from where the kids are at', is an easy way of remembering this important idea.

Adult learning

Educational ideas and practices are often dominated by the needs of children and pedagogy (from the Greek *paidagogia*, 'child-guiding') is the generic term frequently used to describe teaching and learning. However, most teaching in higher education is arguably aimed at young adults and Knowles (1990) has coined the term 'andragogy' (literally 'man-guiding') to refer to this type of teaching and learning. Adults learn in different ways from children, their needs and motivations are different and they approach learning situations with more mature expectations. Adults inevitably think about things differently than children. Importantly they have more life experiences to draw on in discussions or in making decisions or coming to conclusions. Facilitators need to be aware that they are dealing with independent adults and not dependent children. (For more information see p. 160.)

THE NATURE OF GROUPS

Having dealt with some aspects of the nature of individuals that are relevant to the attitudes of SGT facilitators, we shall now consider the nature of groups and the attitudes that facilitators might have towards them.

Kurt Lewin is one of the more important authors to have addressed this problem; his categorization of facilitator behaviour towards groups on the continuum between collaborative and authoritarian gave rise to the three broad descriptions of democratic, autocratic and laissez-faire (Lewin 1952). The authoritarian facilitator basically controls all the objectives and activities of the group and keeps intervening to ensure they are carried out. The laissez-faire facilitator at the other extreme allows the group to decide what its objectives are, what activities it is engaged in and has minimal input into the session. Between these two extremes is the democratic facilitator who collaborates with the group, helping them to agree on a set of objectives and activities and only intervening to keep the group dynamic orientated in a positive direction. On the basis of research on methods of leadership, Lewin found that SGT operated best when conducted in a democratic manner.

However, it is important for facilitators to realize that they may adopt any of these roles in different situations and even during the same session.

John Heron has made an important contribution to the frameworks used to understand the structure and dynamics of SGT with his six dimensions of facilitation model (Heron 1989). According to him facilitators need to be aware of the following basic issues or dimensions which can influence the learning process: planning, meaning, confronting, feeling, structuring and valuing. These are considered to be independent processes that constantly weave through each SGT session. Each dimension has a core question and a 'who decides', 'political' agenda.

■ For the *planning* dimension the key issue is what are the aims of the group and how will they achieve their objectives?

■ The *meaning* dimension is concerned with how meaning should be given to and found in experiences and actions of the group. It is fundamentally concerned with the understanding that is taking place and how the group makes sense of their experiences.

■ The *confronting* dimension concerns itself with how the facilitator deals with resistance, task avoidance and how the group's consciousness can be raised.

■ The *feeling* dimension deals with how the group feelings should be managed.

■ The *structuring* dimension revolves around the types of discussions and activities the facilitator has provided and how the group's learning experiences can be structured.

■ The *valuing* dimension is concerned with how individual autonomy and needs can be acknowledged and supported.

A key issue for facilitators is concerned with who decides on each of these dimensions, the facilitator or the group or a combination of the two. The answer to this question leads to three modes of facilitation for each dimension reminiscent of Kurt Lewin:

■ *hierarchical:* complete facilitator control
■ *co-operative:* shared power with the group
■ *autonomous:* the group decides.

This produces an eighteen block grid of facilitator dimensions and modes through which the effective facilitator moves during a SGT session, as shown in Table 3.1.

Heron concludes by arguing that the most effective facilitator attitude should value autonomy, co-operation and hierarchy in that order as this recognizes the personal autonomy of group members to self-actualize in collaboration with others with the facilitator taking responsibility to achieve group goals.

37

TABLE 3.1 Facilitator dimensions and modes

	Planning	Meaning	Confronting	Feeling	Structuring	Valuing
Hierarchy						
Co-operation						
Autonomy						

COMMUNICATION SKILLS

The ability to listen, respond, explain and question effectively are part of a set of key communication skills that all facilitators of SGT should possess. Questioning is of such importance that it will be dealt with in more detail in the next section.

Active listening

Listening is more than just having a fully functional auditory system that picks up speech. In the same way that merely seeing can be augmented by deliberate, focused observation, hearing the utterances of others can be raised to higher levels by active processes ensuring that all messages are received and that the speaker knows that the message has got through.

There are a number of techniques that SGT facilitators should be aware of. For example, keeping eye contact with a speaker and acknowledging what he or she says by appropriate body language, such as nodding and verbal agreement, is essential for active listening. It is not acceptable to ask a question and then let your attention wander and appear uninterested when someone answers. A further way for facilitators to indicate that they have been actively listening is to summarize or paraphrase what has just been said: 'So what you're saying is . . .'. This is sometimes termed 'reflecting back'.

Responding and explaining

These two communications skills can be dealt with together as they overlap. Facilitators responding to student comments, questions and suggestions should always demonstrate respect, understanding and empathy. If an explanation is required this should use language and concepts that the student will understand. If necessary questions may be asked to clarify the student's understanding and an explanation can then be given at an appropriate level using examples and analogy if appropriate. Further questions can be used to ensure that the student has fully understood.

QUESTIONING

> The questions a teacher asks can make the difference between an antiquated wasteland and an exciting learning environment.
>
> (Carin and Sund 1971: 23)

If active learning is the hallmark of higher educational thinking then the use of questions and questioning skills is the simplest active learning technique. When learners hear a question, they have to think; whether they respond is another matter.

> I keep six honest serving men
> (They taught me all I knew);
> Their names are What and Why and When and How and Where and Who.
>
> (Rudyard Kipling 1912: 43)

The function of questions in SGT

Questions and questioning methods serve a wide variety of functions in SGT and are involved in the following processes:

- arousing interest
- activating prior learning
- diagnosing strengths and weaknesses
- checking progress and understanding
- assessing achievement
- controlling group dynamics by encouraging participation and discussion
- encouraging deep-level thinking and active learning
- reviewing and summarizing.

Arousing interest

Questions at the beginning of a SGT session can arouse interest and motivation. Big questions like 'Do you know what proportion of the

39

UK National Health Service budget is spent on the treatment of diabetes and its complications?' can act as a trigger to generate a whole discussion. After a little thinking time and a few responses, the jaw-dropping correct answer (15 per cent) can act as an extremely powerful stimulus for the relevance and importance of what follows. Each discipline should be able to come up with its own set of 'trigger' questions.

Activating prior learning

Adopting a constructivist and student-centred approach to teaching implies that questions should be used at the beginning of a SGT session to evaluate background knowledge and attitudes and to activate and acknowledge prior learning. Such questions should be mandatory at the beginning of all teaching session but they are especially important in SGT where the aim is to encourage students to talk and discuss.

Diagnosing strengths and weaknesses, checking progress and understanding, and assessing achievement

The responses obtained from individuals after activating prior learning and evaluating background knowledge can be used to diagnose the strengths and weaknesses of the group with respect to the content to be dealt with. The facilitator might then have to briefly review and summarize key points seen as essential for the following discussion or activity if a lack of knowledge is detected. Alternatively, if the group appears knowledgeable, the cognitive level of the work to be carried out could be raised appropriately. Clearly, further questioning during the session can be used to diagnose how well the group is operating and to check understanding. Finally, questioning towards the end of the session can be used to assess how well the group has achieved its learning objectives.

Controlling group dynamics by encouraging participation and discussion

However, one of the most important questioning techniques in SGT is aimed at controlling group dynamics by encouraging participation and discussion. Remember that the initial objective of SGT is to encourage group members to talk and without achieving this none of the other objectives will be achieved. However, questions can often seem intimidating to participants, resulting in an inhibition of participation, so careful consideration needs to be made to the types of questions that are asked and the manner in which they are presented. This is why it is important for a facilitator to be aware of different question types and to know when it is more or less appropriate to use them.

For activating prior learning simple, closed, knowledge recall questions are ideal, initially the simpler the better. After introductions and ice-breaking have been performed, asking questions that students should know the answer to is more likely to encourage a response and even further participation. By gradually introducing more cognitively demanding questions later students will be more likely to respond, whereas if they had been presented earlier they might have resulted in a blank response.

Encouraging deep-level thinking and active learning

The facilitator should be aware of the various cognitive levels of questions and use them appropriately to encourage deep level thinking. Questions aimed at the higher levels, such as analysis or critical evaluation, should be aimed for.

Reviewing and summarizing

Although the facilitator can always review progress and summarize the key learning objectives, a useful technique is to question the group on what they feel they have achieved. Going round the group asking individuals what they feel they have learned or achieved provides an active and participatory closure to the group's activities.

Categories of questions

Questions and questioning techniques can be categorized in a number of ways:

- closed (or convergent) questions
- open (or divergent) questions
- questions aimed at different levels of the learning hierarchy
- probing questions.

These categories are further examined below.

Closed questions

Closed questions are also known as convergent questions as the question is concerned with an item of factual information and homes in or converges on the specific answer. Closed questioning may ask learners to name or identify an object or concept, to define or state a definition of a principle or rule or to compare or contrast two or more processes or systems. The answer to these questions is clearly right or wrong and in fact many closed questions merely involve learners stating yes or no. Closed questions are found at the lowest levels of the cognitive hierarchy and involve simple recall and comprehension. The type of thinking and verbal response elicited involves memory, description, explanation, comparison and illustration. Learners at this level may be asked to explain or illustrate the meaning of key concepts as a way of demonstrating comprehension.

Closed questions are useful in establishing and activating prior learning at the beginning of a SGT session. Because they should be easy to answer they are also useful in warming up learners prior to more complex, open questions.

Examples of closed questions

- What is the name of that bone?
- Define the second law of thermodynamics.
- Who developed the philosophy of dialectical materialism?
- Explain how a . . .
- Compare the two main methods of . . .

Open questions

In most cases open or divergent questions have several possible responses or no fixed response. They may ask learners to defend or justify a particular course of action or moral position. They might involve learners having to apply their knowledge in new, problem-solving or creative situations. They might ask learners to make judgements requiring the use of evidence. They require more elaborate and thoughtful answers and usually cannot be answered by the simple recall of factual information. They elicit and require deep-level thinking involving the higher levels of the cognitive hierarchy. They can involve, for example, application and problem solving in novel situations, analysis of complex concepts, creative speculation, planning and the making of decisions based on the critical evaluation of evidence.

Although a 'big' open-ended rhetorical question is often a useful trigger at the beginning of a SGT session, in terms of questioning dynamics the use of open-ended questions should be reserved for later in the session after the group has been warmed up. Open-ended questions early in a discussion session may be perceived as intimidating and could inhibit participation.

Examples of open questions

- How would you justify making abortion a right of all women?
- What assumptions underpin the abandonment of objective truth in postmodernist thinking?
- How would you make smoking illegal in all public buildings?

In general terms closed questions are aimed at the lower levels of the cognitive hierarchy, whereas open questions are aimed at higher levels. However, the responses obtained from learners are influenced by their degree of competence and experience. In some cases experienced or knowledgeable learners will treat an open ended question as if it were closed. Asking someone in this situation to make a complex judgement or to evaluate evidence may result in the learner simply recalling a predetermined response based on prior knowledge and experience.

Questions aimed at different levels of the learning hierarchy

Bloom's cognitive hierarchy, shown in the left-hand column of Table 3.2, not only is useful in developing learning outcomes for teaching sessions but also can be used to formulate different levels of questions, particularly in the cognitive domain of learning. For most purposes Bloom's six levels are an appropriate framework for thinking about questions.

It can be seen that using questions aimed at different levels of the hierarchy will make students think in different ways, from simple recall through application and up to problem solving and critical evaluation. All SGT facilitators need to be aware of the importance of pushing learners to their cognitive limits, an awareness of questioning levels is very useful in this respect.

■ TABLE 3.2 Questioning at different cognitive levels

Cognitive level	Types of questions	Examples
Evaluation	Questions involving making judgements on the basis of standards, criteria, rules or the critical evaluation of evidence (problem solving)	Judge, defend, evaluate the evidence for, justify
Synthesis	Questions aimed at the creation of new ideas, concepts or plans (problem solving)	Create, speculate, design, plan
Analysis	Questions aimed at analysing assumptions, reasons or evidence (problem solving)	What are the assumptions? What's the evidence? How does this fit together?
Application	Questions aimed at applying or using knowledge in new situations or problems	How would you? What would you do in this situation?
Comprehension	Questions aimed at reformulating or explaining existing knowledge	Compare, contrast, explain, differentiate between
Knowledge	Questions aimed at recalling factual information	What's that called? Define, describe, give me an example of, list some of the causes of

Probing questions

Although SGT facilitators may plan to use specific types of questions at particular points in the session, there will always be situations where additional questions encouraging learners to clarify or elaborate their initial responses are required. These probing questions and questioning sequences can occur in response to open or closed questions or questions directed at different levels of the cognitive hierarchy; they can enable the facilitator to ensure that deep-level understanding is taking place or to diagnose misunderstandings and take appropriate action. Such a sequence of questions might take place after an individual learner has not responded, or responded correctly, incompletely or incorrectly.

Probing questions can be classified into the following types:

- prompting
- justifying
- clarifying
- extending
- redirecting.

Prompting questions

A prompting question is used when a learner does not respond to a question or else gives an incorrect or incomplete answer. The question might contain suggestions or clues, a 'prompt', to the correct answer, hopefully triggering the student to make the necessary response. For example: 'Can't think of anything? Remember last session when we talked about the causes of the First World War . . .' or 'No, pulmonary oedema is associated with the left side of the heart, what about problems with the right side?' or 'That's almost right, but what about the social costs?'

Justifying questions

Justification questions can be used when a learner has provided a correct answer without necessarily explaining why he or she has chosen it. Asking for justification can push learners to the limits of their understanding and is a useful means of diagnosing learners' strengths and weaknesses. For example: 'OK, but which particular category of antibiotic would you use?' or 'Yes, but what's the evidence for that?' or 'But why is it so important to do it that way?'

Clarifying questions

If a student has given a poorly articulated or incomplete answer to a question, clarification can be asked for. Students can be asked to rephrase or elaborate their answer until the facilitator is satisfied that they have answered the question satisfactorily. For example: 'So explain what that means in practice?' or 'Can you be more specific?' or 'Can you rephrase that in non-technical language?'

Extending questions

Superficial understanding is often context dependent whereas deep-level understanding is demonstrated when learners can apply their knowledge to different or new situations. By asking learners to extend and elaborate their thinking to new situations by using extension questions, they

45

are encouraged to think more deeply and their responses give clues to the depth of their understanding. For example: 'How would you modify that treatment if the baby was premature?' or 'Can you give me some examples from the work of Joyce?' or 'If your tax revenue was reduced by one-third what would your priorities be then?'

Redirecting questions

Redirection merely asks the same open-ended questions to different students to generate a variety of responses and to increase participation.

The questioning process

> Humiliation and mental oppression by ignorant and selfish teachers wreak havoc in the youthful mind that can never be undone and often exert a baleful influence in later life.
>
> (Albert Einstein in Calaprice 2000: 69)

As well as having a good working knowledge of questioning types, it is important that the facilitator is also aware of the effects of the questioning process itself on learner behaviour. It has already been mentioned that different types of questions are more likely to elicit a response at different points in a SGT session and can be used to warm students up.

The facilitator's attitude to asking and responding to questions is of crucial importance in creating the right questioning dynamic within the group. Here the ideas and frameworks provided by Rogers, Lewin, Maslow and Heron as discussed previously are important. Combining the conclusions of their work means that facilitators should generate an atmosphere of trust and co-operation where students feel comfortable with asking and responding to questions and where they can feel confident of exposing their lack of knowledge without ridicule or sarcastic comments. This atmosphere is crucially the responsibility of the facilitator, who should warm up the group, set the ground rules and monitor participation and progress. These conditions have already been discussed in Chapter 2 but facilitators should be aware of the anxieties and barriers that students might have when placed in situations where they will be asked questions.

The way in which questions are asked can have a significant impact on whether responses are elicited and their quality. Although in the cut-and-thrust of discussion and debate many questions will be asked, facilitators should try to ensure that their questions are clear and unambiguous. Questions should not be too long nor should they contain too many sub-questions or conditions. They should focus on one fact, idea, concept or problem at a time. Students should be given plenty of 'think time' (at least five seconds and preferably more) to respond before either rephrasing the question or maybe using a prompting question. It is useful to tell students that they are going to have plenty of time to think about their answers. There is evidence (Carin and Sund 1971) that if facilitators leave a long silence after asking a question then students are more likely to respond and even give longer and more elaborate answers.

How the facilitator responds to an answer not only is extremely important to the student answering the question but also sends messages to the rest of the group about how they will be treated if they answer a question. The facilitator should apply active listening skills while listening to the response (see p. 38) and should wait until the complete answer has been given. Then, depending on the answer, an appropriate response should be given. If the answer is correct, this should be acknowledged, with positive and supportive feedback being given. However, if the answer is incorrect or incomplete, some of the probing questioning techniques previously discussed should be used. On no account should the facilitator use negative, sarcastic or personally demeaning language. This does nothing to improve self-esteem or self-confidence and will inhibit participation from the rest of the group.

Summary of recommendations for questioning in SGT sessions

- By appropriate ice-breaking and warming-up, ensure that learners feel comfortable in a questioning environment, exposing their lack of knowledge.
- Use closed questions at the beginning of a session to activate and monitor prior learning and to warm the group up.
- Where possible then use open questions aimed at higher levels of thinking.
- Allow plenty of think time before intervening with more questions.
- Respond to silence or incorrect responses by using prompting questions.
- Do not use sarcastic or hostile responses with learners.
- Respond to correct answers by positive and supportive feedback.

STRUCTURING AND ORGANIZING SGT EXPERIENCES

Like any good teacher, SGT facilitators should have the skills of structuring and organizing a SGT learning experience. They should be aware of the importance of ice-breaking, warming-up and contextualization. They should be skilled in identifying appropriate content and organizing activities, time management and closure. In particular they should have a good knowledge of SGT methods and techniques (see Chapter 4). Many of these skills can be learned only via practice and developed over time, but training programmes should be available to all HE teachers to enable them to learn about and then implement these very important skills.

Management and control

The facilitator has a responsibility to manage and control the work of a SGT group effectively despite the often open-ended and potentially unstructured nature of its work. The facilitator should make clear from the outset, during the introduction or the setting of ground rules, that the session has aims and objectives, a focus on particular activities and a specific structure, and that it has to finish at a particular time. The group should be made aware that they need to talk, discuss, argue and carry out tasks but that these activities are time limited and the facilitator has the right to truncate discussions and activities in order to progress the work of the group and achieve its objectives. In many ways the facilitator performs a balancing act between being autocratic and hierarchical and allowing autonomy and a laissez-faire attitude; they are a benign dictator in charge of the group's freedom

Closure

An important feature of all teaching is closure, where a summary of achieved outcomes can be provided, where conclusions can be emphasized and where learners can be given a sense of accomplishment. This is particularly important in SGT. There should always be time for closure and facilitators should have the time management and control skills to ensure that it takes place. There are a number of ways that closure can be carried out in SGT. The facilitator can keep a note either mentally or on a flip chart of the key points that have arisen and any conclusions

TABLE 3.3 Skills of facilitation in different SGT environments

Type of SGT session	Key facilitator skills required
Group discussion	Producing aims and learning outcomes, warming-up/ice-breaking, questioning, monitoring/time management, summarizing
Group activities	As for 'Group discussion' **plus** clear instructions, appropriate resources, managing task change
Workshops	As for 'Group discussion' **plus** planning, organization, moving from one activity to another, resources, clear instructions
Student-led seminars	Facilitating ground rules, topic identification, resources, clear instructions, giving feedback
PBL	See Chapter 5

that need to be made. These can then be presented at the end using an appropriate medium. Alternatively a member of the group can be given the task of carrying out this activity; this responsibility should be rotated round the group if there are several meetings. A useful technique is to ask the group itself to summarize what they think are the key points learned. This can be done as a specific group activity at the end of the session using a variety of SGT techniques (e.g. pyramids) or alternatively it can be a facilitated discussion, ensuring that all group members have an opportunity to participate (see Table 3.3).

FURTHER READING

Elwyn, G., Greenhalgh, T. and Macfarlane, F. (2001) *Groups: A Guide to Small Group Work in Healthcare, Management, Education and Research*, London: Radcliffe Medical Press.

Jaques, D. (2000) *Learning in Groups: A Handbook for Improving Group Work*, 3rd edn, London: Kogan Page.

Quinn, F. M. (2000) *Principles and Practice of Nurse Education*, Cheltenham: Nelson Thornes.

Westberg, J. and Jason, H. (1996) *Fostering Learning in Small Groups: A Practical Guide*, New York: Springer.

Chapter 4

Working with student groups

Techniques and methods in the classroom

INTRODUCTION

In this chapter we will present and evaluate the effectiveness of a range of group management and facilitation methods. This chapter is intended to give you choice in how you work with a group of students. You will need to make judgements about the appropriateness of various teaching techniques depending upon your own preferred style, the context of the SGT, the specific aims and learning outcomes for the session and the culture of your discipline.

When introducing a new teaching method, do be aware of the expectations of your students and your colleagues. If you are asking your students to work in a new way, you may well need to explain to them why. If you are using a teaching method which is unusual in your department, you may need to be prepared to defend your choice with your colleagues. It is therefore sensible to have teaching intentions that are clearly linked with the learning outcomes and assessments of the course and to have thought through your reasons for selecting particular teaching and learning methods.

It is also important to consider the students you will have in your small group. Do you know if any of your students have special educational needs that might impact on their ability to take a full part in the class? The Special Educational Needs and Disabilities Act (SENDA), which took effect from 1 September 2002, requires that institutions and teachers are *proactive* in seeking to accommodate the needs of their students and in making *reasonable adjustments* to teaching and learning sessions to enable all to learn effectively.

You will need to consider the environment in which the session takes place, the way in which it is structured and delivered and the content of the session itself, in order to ensure disabled students can fully participate. It can be useful to seek suggestions from disabled students themselves, as they are experts on their own disabilities.

(http://www.cowork.ac.uk/development/
materials/seminars/)

There are several sources and web sites that seek to provide more specialist advice on the specific adaptations to teaching that can be beneficial to students with disabilities (please see the further reading at the end of this chapter for some examples, and see Chapter 10 for further discussion of these issues).

STARTING OFF

In Chapter 2, we discussed the reasons for trying to establish a comfortable learning environment and spending time in helping a new group get to know each other. Introductions and breaking the ice can be facilitated in several different ways. You can invite each student to introduce themselves to the whole group in turn, in a 'round'. You can ask them for specific information, e.g. 'Please could you tell us your name and your degree programme and one reason why you chose this module'. Some students will find this nerve-racking, while others will seem to hog the limelight and give you a life history. You may like to indicate your expectations by introducing yourself in the style that you have asked the students to use and so model the level and depth of information you are hoping to get from them. This can take between thirty seconds and one minute per person and so you can calculate the time your introductory round will take.

If time is short and the group is large, you may wish to introduce yourself and then invite the students to introduce themselves to two other people in the room. If you sense your students may be shy talking about themselves, you can ask them to find out about the person sitting next to them and introduce their 'partner' to the group.

WARM-UP AND ICE-BREAKING EXERCISES

You may wish to do more to help the group members get to know each other and establish rapport by organizing an activity specifically

FIGURE 4.1 Breaking the ice

designed to encourage interaction and to help break down the barriers of embarrassment or anxiety in a new group. (see Figure 4.1).

Warming participants up and breaking the ice between them is of great importance if open discussion is to take place quickly. When groups of people who are strangers come together for the first time, there is inevitably a certain level of anxiety. Some people may have had bad experiences of warm-up or ice-breaking exercises that have been perceived as having a high 'cringe factor'. It is the facilitator's responsibility to minimize these problems by using an appropriate activity for the group in hand and by introducing the activity in a non-threatening or embarrassment-provoking way. The tutor also needs to take into account the time an ice-breaking activity will take in session planning.

Some people differentiate between warm-up exercises and ice-breakers; however, there is considerable overlap and they can be thought of as a spectrum of activities ranging from simple introductions at one end to elaborate games and simulations at the other. They are normally used at the beginning of a session when the group forms but they can also be used just after breaks to refocus the group on a new objective or at any time as a way of varying the stimulus and keeping the group active. They can be used to encourage speaking and communication but they can also be used to help group member's work together more easily on problem orientated or creative tasks.

Malseed (1994) suggests they fulfil a variety of functions:

- help break the ice in new groups, by allowing people to learn each other's names and something about each other
- prepare groups for mixing and working together by encouraging, and presenting ways for group members to interact and participate
- wake people up, both physically and mentally, which sharpens their concentration and helps them engage and work more effectively
- help focus groups, both new and established, as preparation for activities to follow, and/or collaborative work
- provide information for facilitators about, for instance, levels of ability and group dynamics, which can valuably inform subsequent planning
- help people have fun and enjoy learning.

A few examples of warm-up exercises and ice-breakers are given below. Further examples can be found in Elwyn *et al.* (2001) whereas Malseed (1994) lists forty-eight activities that have been interestingly categorized into 'low risk', 'medium risk' and 'high risk' in terms of their 'degree of personal risk' to participants.

Low risk activities

- Group members, arranged in a circle, introduce themselves by saying who they are and what name they wish to be called by, what they do for a living or what course they're on, and say something briefly about themselves such as a hobby or interest. The facilitator may prime this process by suggesting that people do not reveal any information about themselves that they don't feel comfortable with the group knowing.
- Group members, arranged in a circle, are asked to form pairs. In pairs, and taking no more than two minutes each, they take turns explaining who they are to their partner

53

giving a brief biography and, for example, ending with something unusual or humorous they have done. Each member of the pair then presents their partner to the group until all have been presented. The facilitator can be included in this process if there is an odd number.

Medium risk activities

- Group members, arranged in a circle, are given a large ball or soft toy. Going round the circle each group member shouts out their name. The person with the ball throws it to someone and shouts the target's name. That person thanks the thrower by name and then throws it to someone else saying their name. If a thrower states a name incorrectly the receiver states their name and throws it back and lets them repeat the correct name. The process continues until everyone has learned everyone else's name.

- Group members, sitting in a circle, are asked to imagine that the space in front of them represents a map with appropriate directions of North, South, East and West. Depending on the background of the group, the map could represent the whole of the Earth, one continent or one country. Participants are then asked to position themselves approximately at the location of their birth on the imagined map. Once they have agreed on their positions the facilitator asks everyone in turn to tell the group their birth location and first name plus something about its origin, meaning or family history. Next group members are asked to move to a position where they went to school, university or any other learning institution. When they have moved again in turns, they are asked to tell the group what they studied at this location. Participants then return to their seats in the circle.

Higher risk activities

- Group members are issued with a list of, for example, ten facts about a person with a space next to each one for a name to be written. The list might include facts such as, 'Is an only child', 'Is an eldest child', 'Has visited the USA', 'Is a Manchester United supporter', 'Hates opera', 'Has done a parachute jump' etc. Group members now mingle and ask each other questions until as many of the spaces as possible are filled up. In this process everyone talks to everyone else and finds out their name.

■ Group members are paired up and given three pieces of A4 paper, a pair of scissors, three strips of adhesive tape and a can of baked beans. Each pair has twenty minutes to support the can of beans, using the paper, as high as possible above a desk for at least ten seconds.

FINDING OUT MORE ABOUT THE STUDENTS

With a new group you may wish to find out more about your students at the start of the class. They may have studied different courses before joining your module, they may have different special needs, and they may come from different countries and cultures. The diversity in the class can be used very beneficially to broaden and deepen discussion and learning.

You can simply ask your students about their prior learning in the topic or discipline and that is likely to give you a quick overview of their experience and what they have studied in the past. However, such an approach may tell you less about the abilities of the class. You can also use a quiz or set of short questions or problems to help you find out more. Although the use of a 'pre-test' can provide much useful information for the tutor, it does need to be used sensitively. Some students will feel very anxious if your test feels like an exam. Therefore, you need to think carefully about how you introduce the test or quiz and how you handle the results. If you use the quiz to structure your first discussion, you can avoid much of the anxiety. For example, give ten short questions to the group asking them about the topics that you will be studying together. Try to mix your questions so that you can find out what they are already familiar with and how far they are able to use (e.g. analyse, interpret etc.) their knowledge. Then go through the responses to each question in class, asking the group for their answers and reactions. Alternatively you could read out the answers and ask them to mark their own and then, with a neighbour, come up with three questions that they would like to ask about the test. In both scenarios you will indirectly be able to find out more about the current level and abilities of your class. You will achieve this without creating greater anxiety for your new students and avoiding the extra work that would arise if you took in answer sheets to mark yourself.

55

Many first-year students may come to university without having experienced a tutorial or seminar before. The question 'How are we going to work together?' may never have been asked of them before. So it may be very worthwhile to use some of your first meeting with a new group of students to find out about their expectations and clarify the working relationship between 'tutor and students' and 'students and students'. The development and use of ground rules was discussed in Chapter 2; certainly they provide an excellent vehicle for negotiating and agreeing roles, responsibilities and how the class will operate. A colleague in economics begins each tutorial with a new group of students by writing on the board two questions, 'How do you think we will work together in the tutorial?' and 'What should the tutor do?' He then makes some excuse to leave the room for a couple of minutes and then (usually) rejoins a lively discussion back in the classroom. At this point he can ask what the group thinks and he can add his own views and put right any misconceptions that he finds.

ACTIVE SGT TASKS

Let us now assume the group has been formed and students and tutor know the aims and learning outcomes for the session. At the heart of SGT is the active involvement in tasks and activities that lead to greater understanding, learning and the development of skills. Here are some ways in which you can structure and manage discussions and activities in the classroom.

Rounds

As with the introductory round described earlier, here the students are asked to respond in turn and all are involved and contributing. Rounds work best when the seating arrangements allow participants to see each other when they are talking and when the number of students in the group is fewer than sixteen. Above this number, the round can become too time-consuming and laboured. Rounds can be used at the start of a session to provide a realistic focus or to check current levels of understanding, e.g. please complete the following sentence in turn, 'A good teacher tries to'. Or let us produce a joint list of 'Things that help me learn.'

During a session a round can be used to collect examples or to provide students with an opportunity to ask questions, e.g. 'In a round let us collect examples of people who are leaders', or alternatively, 'One thing I am not sure about is'.

At the end of a SGT session you can use a round to help bring a session to a close and relate the learning outcomes back to the learner through an active summary or action plan, e.g. 'One thing I learnt today is' or 'What I will do next is'.

Pass the pen

This is a modification of the 'round' technique which asks the students to jointly compile a list of contributions and write up their point before passing the pen to the next person in line or a person of their choice. International students, for whom English is not their first language, or very shy students, may find this form of written communication easier to enter into than the usual verbal forms.

Choose an item

A further adaptation of the 'round' is to provide several items and ask the students to choose one and talk about it for a minute or to present the pros and cons of using it, or to place in priority order etc.

The items might be archaeological specimens or pieces of medical equipment or poems, whatever makes sense for the discipline. The students may feel that some items are easier to talk about than others and there might be a rush to choose first and get the best items. Alternatively you manage the choice so that your students take it in turns or get the opportunity to choose when they have completed another task.

Brainstorming

Brainstorming is a very useful and popular SGT activity that can be traced back to the work of Osborne in the 1930s (Osborne 1957) where it was used to stimulate groups to generate a range of ideas, options and creative suggestions in a non-judgemental atmosphere. Not only can it achieve specific content orientated goals but also it can be used as a warm-up exercise and ice-breaker.

A brainstorm has two distinct parts. During part one the focus should be on *quantity* rather than *quality* and the aim is to generate lots of ideas and encourage lateral thinking. The tutor, or one of the students, should list the ideas and comments as they are put forward by the students.

During this 'creative' phase you should not stop the flow of new ideas by discussing or questioning any of the contributions. Then in part two of the brainstorm you move to analyse and evaluate the list of suggestions that has been produced. So rather than critiquing an individual's contribution you view the list as a product to be collectively studied further. During part two the group uses your guidance and directions to begin to rule out and rule in contributions, to group items and to consider their interrelationship and relative importance. For example, you may suggest that the students view the list in terms of 'urgent' and 'important' or 'immediate, short-term and long-term strategies'.

Separating the two phases has the impact of freeing discussion and enabling the students to make more original and unguarded points. It is therefore an excellent approach to adopt when problem solving or designing. The class dynamics are also worth commenting on. The high energy of a brainstorm can be used to 'wake-up' tired students or open up a new topic in the middle of a SGT session. This can be an excellent way of including variety in a session to change pace and process.

Mind maps and topic maps

Also used as writing techniques to help overcome writers' block, mind mapping can be used to good effect by a group to solve problems, work creatively and explore new topics in a SGT session. Originated in the late 1960s by Tony Buzan, mind maps are a visual method of generating and seeing relationships between ideas, concepts and things (Buzan 1993). Mind maps enable participants to see the key relationships between concepts in a specific subject area, helping them to gain an overview that is helpful in organizing their learning. They can help to break down the relationships between ideas and expose their underlying assumptions, they help to create new relationships between ideas and they can help learners explore how they construct their own mental models.

The process involves the tutor writing up the topic to be addressed in the middle of the blackboard (or white-board or flip chart) and then inviting the group members to think of points that come to mind when considering the topic. The contributions are written up on the board using a series of interconnecting lines to indicate the relationships between points. For example, contributions may be grouped together in a sub-set of related points or consumed within a major topic and represented by sub-branching lines moving outwards from the main topic. As with the brainstorm described earlier, you may wish to divide the process into two clear parts: first, generate lots of ideas, second, analyse the mind map and further critique the contributions. The advantages of such an approach are that all the students can take part and the end product of their collaboration can then be used by all to help structure the further study of the topic. You may also want to suggest that your students could use the same technique to help them get started on their individual writing assignments?

SWOT analysis

SWOT stands for strengths, weaknesses, opportunities and threats. It is an analysis technique that can be used within a group to review their own progress on a joint project. For example, a student team preparing to work on a multidisciplinary project in engineering could use a SWOT analysis to help them identify and address the issues facing the group. The analysis can highlight the 'What do we need to do to work together effectively?' questions, as differences in approach can become a problem for the group (and the tutor). A SWOT can also be used by the students in a tutorial when they are evaluating case studies, e.g. in business studies students could be asked to consider the current state of a particular company using a SWOT analysis and make recommendations on the next steps that company should take.

SWOT analysis is also a SGT technique that is ideally suited to managing change. It can be used, for example, when new working practices are being proposed or when a new curriculum is being introduced. It enables participants to openly acknowledge their strengths and weaknesses when dealing with the proposed change and to speculate on the opportunities that the change might provide as well as the perceived threats.

It can be carried out with a standard sized small group or with a larger group that is divided up into smaller groups. In the latter case one facilitator can run the whole event provided each group has a leader who can keep to the agenda.

The technique will be described for use with multiple groups. The SWOT analysis might begin by a general plenary introduction where the nature of the proposed change is outlined to participants and where the overall SWOT process is described. Briefly groups are expected to brainstorm on each of the four headings and then refine and summarize their findings for presentation in a plenary session at the end. Participants

59

should be in no doubt what they are expected to do and to achieve and should be aware of the timescale involved. The facilitator should split the group into smaller groups of about eight members. A variety of techniques can be used to do this depending on the agenda.

There are two ways multiple groups can perform a SWOT analysis, the amount of time available being the deciding factor. If there are four groups or more each group can deal with a specific section of the SWOT analysis. It may mean that there is some duplication of headings but that is not necessarily a problem. Alternatively each group deals with each heading in turn. Clearly the latter case will require more time than the former. Before each group begins they should engage in a brief ice-breaking and introduction activity and the choosing or volunteering of a leader, who will act as a chairperson and keep the group on task. The facilitator may come round and visit each group in turn during this process to ensure the task is being carried out correctly and to co-ordinate timing. Each segment of the SWOT analysis should be recorded either on a flip chart or an overhead transparency for later presentation.

Once the SWOT analysis has been completed, the groups should come together for a plenary at which each group's findings are presented. The facilitator then leads a discussion with the aim of coming up with a summary of the whole group's views on their strengths and weaknesses and the opportunities and threats they perceive. However, this should then lead on to the creation of a list of priority issues and action points. This may be carried out as a large group activity, or if there is time, the groups may split up once again to discuss and then present their conclusions.

The outcomes of an effective SWOT analysis should lead towards a consensus on how to proceed and an action plan. In principle the facilitator should act as an independent arbiter of the process to allow the groups to achieve their own consensus. It would not be appropriate for the facilitator to be pushing any particular agenda. The facilitator should also be aware that various degrees of conflict might arise and should be prepared to deal with them.

Buzz groups and pyramids

A buzz group, so called because of the level of noise that explodes in the room, is when two or three students are asked to discuss a question or topic for a few moments. The level and pitch of the question is important. It should be about something that all the students can sensibly discuss, either from their own experience or from their learning on the course. In setting questions it may help to precede the buzz group by giving the students a few seconds to write down their own response before being asked to discuss it with a colleague. More of the students will take part in this preparation phase if you attach a quantitative goal, for example, 'Please write down five reasons to give a lecture' or 'In priority order, list three causes of chest pain'. This would then be followed by instructions such as, 'Please compare your list with two people sitting next to you' or 'Look over at your neighbour's list and see if you agree'.

The main reasons for asking students to work in this way is to encourage them to think about the topic for themselves and to get all the students actively engaged. A secondary reason may be to collect the views or answers from the students and incorporate their responses in the whole class discussions. If this is an aim then you will need to take feedback from the students. Please see the section on 'Getting feedback: hearing back from the students' (p. 69) for some suggestions on how to do this.

However, it is worth mentioning here that you are much more likely to get feedback from the students if you have asked them to discuss their ideas with another student first. Students who have spoken and had the chance to rehearse their views in private are then much more likely to speak in public. During a buzz group they have also had the opportunity to get their points of view reinforced (or challenged) so that it is no longer just their idea but a peer has supported it. Again this is encouragement to 'risk' bringing their point forward into the class discussion.

Students who have discussed a question in pairs can then be asked to join with another pair and extend their conversations and deepen their exploration of the topic. This group of four could then be invited to join with another four and combine their thinking and negotiate a group response. This is sometimes called 'pyramiding' or 'snowballing' and can be a structured way of forming larger groups or syndicate groups in which you can be sure that everybody has had the opportunity to express their thoughts even if they would normally be inhibited in a group of eight people. One drawback of this technique is that participants may find themselves repeating points initially made in the pair, in the four and then again in the eight. For this reason we do not recommend that this technique is used frequently as it may lead to some students feeling frustrated and bored.

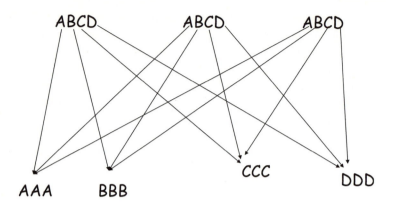

FIGURE 4.2 The technique of cross-grouping

Cross-over and mixed groups

A class can be divided into groups of four students to work together on a problem or discussion topic. Rather than reporting their findings back to plenary, the tutor can ask, for example, two students from one group to swap places with two students from another group and so 'cross-over'. Here the intention is that ideas generated in one group can be added to those produced in another group and so 'grow' the topic and broaden the debate. One way for the tutor to manage a cross-over activity is illustrated in Figure 4.2.

Initially each member is given a code number that represents their membership of the first group and their membership of the second group. For example if there are to be initially four groups of three then participants can be labelled as 'A', 'B', 'C' or 'D'. Participants would then be asked to form three groups, ensuring that there was an 'A', a 'B', a 'C' and a 'D' in each one. They would then engage in some appropriate activity for a specific amount of time. Groups would be crossed over by asking four new groups to form such that all the 'As' were together, all the 'Bs' and so on. The new groups would then carry out the next part of the activity.

Cross-grouping is very useful for facilitating small groups working together on different tasks, the results of which can finally be reported in the whole group. This process means that participants first have to collaborate to achieve the first outcome and then, after the cross-over, they have to present and explain what they have achieved to the members of another group, who may question them to clarify points. A large amount of content can be covered in this process with all participants learning by collaboration, by presenting, by listening and questioning. Cross-grouping can be time managed in a single SGT session but the first phase could also be an extensive piece of collaborative work involving additional self-directed learning and presentation preparation.

However, as with the pyramid approach discussed previously, there is a danger that some students may feel that the technique in practice causes them to repeat or hear again previously discussed ideas. A slight adaptation of the basic technique can help to avoid this situation: the problem or topic is divided into two or more stages and the cross-over occurs as the students move from one level to the next. The focus of the discussion is moving on and repetition is avoided while still gaining some of the benefits of having a remixed group.

A variation on this approach can be used in quantitative problem classes when students are asked to solve mathematical or statistical problems. The tutor can take one group of students through a solution to check their understanding and the accuracy of their working-out and final answer. These students can then join other groups and act as student tutors for that problem. The tutor can then check the solution for a second problem with a second group of students, who will then act as student tutors for this second problem and help their peers. There is growing evidence that such peer tutoring is not only helpful for the students who get help but also helpful for the student tutor who gains a greater depth of understanding through the process of teaching.

Cut-ups, cards and Post-its

It is possible to encourage group discussion and deep-level thinking by utilizing paper-based resources in sequencing, assembling, categorizing and prioritizing activities. These techniques can be inserted into any SGT session to vary the stimulus and encourage further interactivity. They can also be fun!

Cut-ups involve cutting up lists of ideas, concepts, processes, definitions, statements, names, dates and so on, placing them in an envelope and giving them to a small group of two or three students. The students are then given instructions on how they are to process what they have been given, ranging from specific to open-ended. For example they might be given no instructions at all and have to decide what to do from the context of the SGT session. Alternatively they may be asked to categorize them in a particular way, placing them in related groups.

63

Or they might have to put them into a prioritized list or a logical sequence. For example, the tutor provides envelopes containing cut-ups on different coloured paper where the task is to match or relate the contents of one envelope with another. Examples could include 'A problem and possible solutions', 'A disease and treatments', 'A chemical and its mode of synthesis', etc. The technique is limited only by the imagination of the facilitator.

Sets of cards containing information printed on sticky labels are also a useful resource for SGT. Again they can contain ideas, concepts, processes, definitions, statements, names, dates or any information that is relevant to the task in hand. Students can use the cards in a variety of ways: as stimuli for discussion; as partial lists that need to be completed; as steps in a process.

Coloured Post-its are a flexible resource, which enable students to move ideas around and to examine relationships between them. Students can write on them, stick them on a flip chart or white-board and then rearrange them according to the activity being undertaken. Post-its are very useful for getting students to create mind maps (see p. 58).

When students engage in these activities, they immediately start talking to each other, discussing their reasons and choices for categorization or sequencing and arguing to support particular outcomes. Depending on the nature of the task this can lead to deep-level thinking and a critical evaluation of concepts and relationships. Afterwards in the larger group, by encouraging participants to reflect on how they came to their decisions, further elaboration of ideas and metacognition can be achieved.

Syndicate groups

Most of the common difficulties faced when facilitating SGT sessions, e.g. quiet groups or shy students, over-talkative individuals and mixed abilities, can be minimized if the small group is made smaller. Using small working groups or syndicate groups to research or discuss issues or work through problem sheets together is a common approach that can be very effective in a wide range of situations. The syndicate group method can be used within a small or a large group class or be used to support independent study and homework assignments that may follow-on from the class.

If facilities are available, syndicate SGT can begin with the class meeting together to be given the work tasks and then quickly dividing off into different rooms for the majority of the class time. The tutor would move between the groups to answer questions or prompt further discussion and understanding. The tutor may also be monitoring and checking that the students are doing what they are supposed to be doing. The class would come back together for the last ten minutes of the session to report back and hear from the tutor who may, depending on the learning outcomes and discipline, summarize the key points, indicate common mistakes or distribute answer sheets and further reading lists.

MORE ADVENTUROUS TECHNIQUES

The techniques considered here require advanced planning and the development of appropriate learning resources. While the use of role-play and simulations is commonplace in some academic disciplines, their adoption is by no means universal. Tutors should be sensitive to the local culture of their teaching environment and aim to lessen anxiety if teaching approaches go beyond the normal experience of students. For example, a tutor may wish to introduce a role-play as a 'chance to practise' or a simulation as a 'worked case study' if the words 'role-play' and 'simulation' are likely to cause undue trepidation in themselves.

Fish-bowling

Fish-bowling, as the name implies, involves having one group observe a smaller group working within it (see Figure 4.3). For example, it could involve a large group observing a smaller group of seven or eight engaging in problem based learning or a guided discussion. Alternatively it could involve a group observing a role-play of an interview or a simulated consultation. However, fish-bowling is more than just observation. The tutor may stop the activity of the smaller group for several minutes and invite comments or suggestions from the larger group. The facilitator might encourage or specifically direct the larger group to observe the interpersonal dynamics, the strategies used or the questioning approaches occurring within the smaller group and may encourage discussion on these areas. The smaller group more or less ignores the comments from the larger group and its members do not participate in the larger group discussion. At a signal from the facilitator, the smaller group continues its activity. This starting and stopping process can occur several times during the session.

65

FIGURE 4.3 Fish-bowling

Role-play

Role-play is an extremely powerful way of encouraging small group participants to explore their own behaviour and the behaviour of others in simulated situations. Properly used it enables participants to analyse their attitudes and behaviour, to obtain feedback on their behaviour and try out different behaviours (Holsbrick-Engels 1994). For group members whose objectives are concerned with the development of interpersonal relationships and communication skills, role-play is a very powerful learning experience. However, because of its power, it is a potentially dangerous technique that can be emotionally distressing for unprepared participants. Facilitators should use it with care and with proper preparation and monitoring.

Basically role-play involves asking someone to be someone else, to pretend to be another person in an imagined situation; it is acting or improvising without a script. Usually this takes place in front of the rest of the group during a fish-bowling activity (see previous section). Clearly, very powerful experiential learning can occur for the role-play participants but it can be an equally powerful learning experience for the observers, which can be reinforced if appropriate questioning and debriefing is undertaken by the facilitator.

Many types of role-play revolve around the interaction between two people and hence two participants are required for such situations. For example:

- doctor–patient
- lawyer–defendant
- mother/father–son/daughter
- parent–teacher
- researcher–supervisor/industrialist
- social worker–client
- teacher–student
- trainer–trainee
- manager–employee
- tutor–tutee
- designer–client
- shop assistant–customer
- waiter–diner.

More elaborate situations can involve more people, leading to simulations of quite complex interpersonal interactions.

Elwyn *et al.* (2001) claim that the benefits of role-play derive from its immediacy and its ability to bring learning to life in a safe environment. They suggest that role-play helps participants to

- express hidden feelings and discuss sensitive problems
- understand how others feel and react in different situations
- observe how some people handle complex, difficult social situations
- become completely engaged with and captivated by an issue or idea
- receive immediate and diverse feedback about their performance
- close the gap between 'theory' and 'practice' and consolidate skill development
- change their attitudes.

However, many people have anxieties about participating in role-play. It is often seen as embarrassing for both role-players and observers. Some people feel shy about acting in front of other people or feel vulnerable about exposing their attitudes and behaviours in public. Some people see role-play as a trivial waste of time. It is the facilitator who has to deal with these negative issues and who must set the situation up in such a way as to reduce anxiety and to ensure participants see the benefits to be obtained. Preparation and priming is all if role-play is to work successfully. For example, a role-play should fit within the over-all outcomes of a SGT session. Participants should be fully informed of what to expect and if necessary appropriate volunteers should be re-cruited. Role-players should be briefed on what their roles are by giving them pre-printed role descriptions or by providing a written scenario describing the situation they are supposed to be in. The role-play should be timed and monitored.

The standard technique for using a role-play would be for it to be introduced, carried out and then discussed by the group. However, Van Ments has described a number of variations that can be introduced into the proceedings (Van Ments 1989).

- *Role reversal:* participants can swap roles, for example a trainer can become a trainee. This is particularly useful for allowing participants to explore how they feel.
- *Role rotation:* the main role (for example a manager) is rotated through the participants so that everyone has an experience of the role.
- *Alter ego:* a participant stands behind the main role-player and acts as his or her alter ego or alternative self, voicing the role-player's imagined thoughts or feelings in the first person such as 'I was hurt by that remark'. The alter ego may also act to move the role-play on if the role-player gets stuck and can't think of anything to say.
- *Replay:* used by the facilitator to allow the role-players to 'rewind' and act out a specific sequence again. The facilitator may also pause proceedings to allow the observers to make comments on what they see happening (see 'Fish-bowling', p. 65).
- *Fast-forward:* if the facilitator feels that time is running out or that a particular issue has now been dealt with they can 'fast-forward' to a later situation in the role-play.

Once a role-play has been completed it is traditional for the role-players to formally close down their roles and re-establish their own identities by stating who they are. This may require a few moments if the situation has been an emotional one or students have been asked to embody viewpoints with which they fundamentally disagree. The next phase is to engage the whole group in a debrief where the role-play is analysed, discussed, dissected and the learning points extracted.

Simulations and games

Simulations and games can be designed to provide learners with opportunities to explore some aspect of the real world in the safety and relative simplicity of a SGT environment. There are a great variety of simulations and games available right across the higher education curriculum (see the Society for the Advancement of Games and Simulations in Education and Training (SAGSET) web site: http://www.ms.ic.ac.uk/sagset/). Simulations may be introduced into the curriculum to try to provide students with a learning experience that may otherwise be denied them because of the cost, feasibility, safety etc. Simulations may also be used to give the students additional opportunities for preparation, practice or review, if providing lots of the 'real thing' is difficult or impossible.

Games involve participants by using active, highly motivating and memorable methods of learning. Calling a learning activity a game reduces the personal cost for many students but may also reduce the appreciation of the learning taking place, so the tutor's role is often to reinforce and underline the points that emerge from the experience.

GETTING FEEDBACK: HEARING BACK FROM THE STUDENTS

If students have been asked to work in smaller groups or syndicate groups during part of the class, there is often a need to bring the class back together in plenary to share learning and outcomes. This is often referred to as 'taking feedback' and there are several ways that this can be managed. The choice of approach clearly depends upon the initial learning outcomes for the class but may also depend on the amount of time available.

If time is short the tutor may simply want to sample students' work to get an impression of their discussions. By simply asking groups to report back one point from their discussions ('The most important, the point you spent the longest discussing' etc.). However, in many cases the tutor will want a fuller report back from syndicate work.

69

The danger of pointing the finger

If you 'pick on' students and put them on the spot to answer a question or feedback, you may be lucky and ask a confident student who has a helpful response at the ready and all may go well. However, you run the risk of getting embarrassed silence, a muddled and unfocused response or at worst a very upset and discouraged student. Why take this risk? After all it is the tutor who then has to rescue the situation and rebuild the atmosphere in the classroom. This approach can work well for some tutors but for many of us it is actually a sign that we haven't properly prepared and fully thought through how we would prefer to get student feedback. It can often be a somewhat desperate act in order to get students to talk to us and can backfire horribly.

Instant posters

Asking students to work together to list their responses on a sheet of flip chart paper can be a helpful way to give a clear focus to their group's discussions or problem solving. As the group is working it also gives the tutor a visible means of monitoring progress and the direction the discussion has taken. Once the work is completed the poster can be the sole means of feedback if time is short. It can be very interesting to put up the posters on the wall and ask small groups to read each other's feedback.

Alternatively you could invite a group spokesperson to pick out two key points from their poster and continue in this way for each group to gain further insight into the detail of their internal discussions. Or you could ask for a full verbal report back to accompany the poster from one group and then ask for additional comments or questions from the other groups.

Using Post-its and overhead transparencies

While instant posters can work very well for a group feedback situation the smaller scale offered by self-adhesive Post-it notes or individual sheets of acetate to be viewed on the overhead projector (OHP) can better provide an appropriate medium for collecting a range of individual (or pair's) responses. For example, a tutor may say to a class towards the end of the third SGT session with them:

Please could you give me some feedback on how you think these classes are going and how could we improve them for you? I am sending around the class a pack of Post-it notes and I would like you each to take two. On one please write *I would like you to continue* . . . and on the second please write *I would like you to stop* . . .

Using overhead transparencies for feedback can provide an opportunity to show a range of student views together. For example, the tutor can cut a sheet of acetate into quarters and give each pair or small group a pen and a piece of acetate each. Then ask each group to list the three words that best describe 'X' for them, or their estimated cost of 'X', or the main symptoms of 'X' (or some other appropriate short feedback response) on the acetate. The tutor can then display up to four responses together and draw comparisons between them in a summarizing discussion. This feedback technique also has the advantage that the tutor gets to see all of the students' responses before they are displayed to the whole group. The tutor can therefore choose to group similar responses or juxtapose student views in their presentation of acetates. The tutor can also begin to formulate a reaction to the student 'voice' and, if necessary, to provide a final summary to include any absent key points and to correct any errors in understanding made by the students.

Nominated spokesperson

When syndicate groups have completed a task, they may be invited to report back to plenary through a group spokesperson. It is helpful if tutors can give very clear instructions about how they would like the spokesperson to do this. For example: 'Please nominate a spokesperson to feed back the best and worst example you came up with in your group' or 'Please give a two minute report back summarizing your discussions using a poster'.

It may be a good idea to ask the group to choose a spokesperson when they are nearing the completion of the work task, as the selecting of the spokesperson can become a time-consuming job if you let it.

Student presentations

Students can be asked to prepare a more formal report-back presentation on their work either individually, in pairs or as a group. Asking students to talk to the whole group can be a very daunting prospect for many and this should be handled with care and consideration. In Chapter 6 we will look in more detail at the approaches used in 'student-led' seminars and how to help your students develop their presentation and facilitation skills. Here, it is enough to say that you should try to see presenting to the group as part of a continuum in which the students can first be asked to express themselves to a partner, then to a small private group, then briefly to the whole group. Rather than throwing your students into the deep end and asking them, straight away, to give a formal, ten-minute presentation to the whole class, work up to this and your students will gain in skill; more importantly they will gain in confidence.

See Chapter 6 for further techniques and methods that can be used by tutors and student seminar leaders to organize and structure class discussions including the use of debates, triggers and stimuli, vignettes and case studies, role-play and quizzes.

EXAMPLES FROM DIFFERENT DISCIPLINES

Here are some selected examples of class plans that indicate the timings and methods chosen from a range of different subjects. In these examples a number of graduate teaching assistants and lecturers explain how they organize some of their classes in their own subjects.

Law

In my classes, I divide the students into two groups that usually consist of six students per group. I prepare two essay questions, one giving a particular standpoint and the other with the opposite standpoint. The idea behind the two questions is that each group must defend their particular standpoint. I ask all the students to pre-prepare four or five points that will illustrate their argument individually. At the beginning of each class I leave the students for about ten to fifteen minutes to discuss the question they have been allocated and to come up with four or five points collectively to support their standpoint. I have found that this works much better if I leave the room, as they are less inhibited and more inclined to talk. This also works well because even if a particular student has not prepared, he or she can then get some ideas from the other students. I have found that the other students will force the student who does not prepare to do some work as the rest will tire of someone who consistently does not do their share. We then spend about twenty to thirty minutes debating both questions as a whole group and summarize at the end with a vote on which of the questions they most agreed with. I sometimes also summarize the main points in the discussion.

Statistics

In my problems class the course leader provides a list of problems to the students at the end of their lecture the week before. We then have fifty minutes to go through them together. The students are told to work through them before they come to class and some of them have, but some of them haven't. I have found that there are too many questions to go through in the time available so I ask the students at the beginning if they have any questions and which of the problems they have struggled with. We draw up a list of questions together and this takes about five to ten minutes. I then begin to go through a question writing up the solution line by line on the overhead projector. I stop frequently to ask the group questions; they know I don't mind if they get it wrong and so are quite willing to shout out answers. This can take about ten to fifteen minutes as I try to draw out pointers that will help them with some of the other questions. Having gone through one question in this way, I then ask the students to work in pairs to look at the next question(s) together and I work around the pairs helping them when they get stuck. They do really help each other and I find that lots of the little questions get sorted out before I get to them. If I find that several people are having difficulty with a particular question, I may ask one or two of the students (who I know have got it right) to show the rest of the class their worked solutions on the board. This is especially interesting if they have tackled the problem in different ways and we can discuss the pros and cons of different methods. I finish the class with a final Any Questions round but usually by then we have sorted out most of the concerns.

Economic history

Two of the students are asked to pre-prepare the answer to a question based on their readings of three or four articles or chapters. They formally present this to the class – I ask them to spend about ten minutes presenting their argument. While they are doing this I come up with a suitable question that arises from their presentation. It may be about something that they have not fully explained or an assumption that they have pushed too far. I then divide the class up into work groups of about four students and ask them to tackle the question together for about twenty minutes. I leave them on their own for about ten minutes, to avoid leading or directing them too much at the start, then I join the groups one by one. I then try to guide them in their consideration of the question and prompt them to be more rigorous with their treatment of models and data. We then come back together as the whole class (about sixteen) and I will ask a couple of the groups to respond to the question and ask the other students to ask them questions and comment on each other's answers. If necessary I finish the class with a quick round-up of key issues or main points but often this is not needed as the students have identified them during discussion.

Astronomy and physics: role-playing exercises

In these exercises, I divided my class into small teams typically of three students. Each team is then given a briefing paper, describing some facet of a particular astronomical mystery. The teams have to wander around the classroom, exchanging information with other groups, until they can piece together a complete solution to the astronomical mystery. They can then present their solution and win a prize.

The exercises have been run successfully in classes as large as 150 students, and as small as 12 students. I see no reason why they should not work equally well in larger classes still. They have been run with students as young as Year 10 (aged 14–15 years) and as old as graduate students. To find out more see the electronic paper by P. J. Francis and A. P. Byrne at http://www.atnf.csiro.au/pasa/16_2/francis/paper/

FURTHER READING

Baume, D. and Baume, C. (1996) *Learning to Teaching: Running Tutorials and Seminars – Training Materials for Research Students*, Oxford: Oxford Centre for Staff Development.

Elwyn, G., Greenhalgh, T. and Macfarlane, F. (2001) *Groups: A Guide to Small Group Work in Healthcare, Management, Education and Research*, Oxford: Radcliffe Medical Press.

Jaques, D. (2000) *Learning in Groups*, 3rd edn, London: Kogan Page.

Northedge, A. and the H851/HH851 course team (1998) *Practice Guide 1: Teaching in Groups*, OU Series H851 Teaching in HE: theory and evidence, Milton Keynes: The Open University.

USEFUL WEB SITES

http://cti-psy.york.ac.uk/aster/ ASTER Project, *Small-Group Teaching and C&IT*. This site provides information and resources to support the use of communication and information technologies in small-group teaching and learning (accessed 9 June 2003).

http://www.mind-map.com/index.htm Buzan Centres, Mind Maps (accessed 9 June 2003).

http://www.leeds.ac.uk/disabilityservices/information/staffinfo.html Disability Services, University of Leeds, Information for Staff Pages provide useful information on adapting teaching to better suit the needs of disabled students (accessed 9 June 2003).

http://www.brookes.ac.uk/services/ocsd/2_learntch/small-group/ sgtindex.html Jacques, D., *Small Group Teaching*, Oxford Centre for Staff and Learning Development, Oxford Brookes University (accessed 9 June 2003).

http://www.cdtl.nus.edu.sg/Ideas/iot9.htm Mohanan, K. P., *Small Group Teaching in Large Classes*, Centre for Development of Teaching and Learning (CDTL), National University of Singapore (accessed 9 June 2003).

http://medical.faculty.ncl.ac.uk/schools/medev/cpd/staff_dev/ sd14_groupteach Small Group Teaching, School of Medical Education Development, University of Newcastle upon Tyne (accessed 9 June 2003).

http://www.ms.ic.ac.uk/sagset/ Society for the Advancement of Games and Simulations in Education and Training (SAGSET) (accessed 9 June 2003).

Chapter 5

Problem based learning

INTRODUCTION

Problem based learning is a SGT technique increasingly being used in a wide variety of subject areas in higher education. In this chapter we begin by examining what PBL is, how it is used and the facilitator skills required to run a PBL session. For people interested in introducing PBL into their teaching, and because of its controversial nature, we will also look at some of the evidence for its effectiveness as an educational tool. Finally, we will look at some examples of PBL in different disciplines.

WHAT IS PBL?

Problem based learning is essentially a SGT method that has been developed and expanded into being a major way for learners to acquire the knowledge, skills and attitudes of a significant proportion of a course or curriculum. However, it should be remembered that the term PBL has been used in a variety of ways in the literature and more recently the term 'enquiry based learning' has also been used (see web sites in Further reading). In a review of the field Vernon and Blake (1993) showed that it has been used to refer to a general teaching philosophy, a particular use of learning objectives and goals or an overall view of educational attitudes and values. Walton and Matthews (1989) describe three characteristics of PBL that help to differentiate it from more traditional teaching approaches. First, the curriculum organization revolves around problems rather than disciplines and there is emphasis on integrated learning and the overt development of cognitive skills as well as understanding. Second, it is dominated by active

SGT methods and independent learning. Third, one of its aims is the development of lifelong learning attitudes. In this chapter we will describe a common and generic type of PBL. You can use the references to find out more information about different variants on the basic theme.

As Barrows and Tamblyn (1980: 12) state, PBL is 'the learning which results from the process of working towards the understanding of, or resolution of, a problem.' As will be discussed later, there are many different variants of PBL but what PBL is *not* is merely teaching using problems as examples or giving students problems to solve. Problem solving in the latter context is concerned with learning problem-solving techniques or finding the answers to a problem. Although these are laudable educational goals, they do not match up to the much more elaborate outcomes of PBL.

PBL is concerned with working and learning in collaborative and highly motivated groups where communication and interpersonal skills are developed, personal and group learning objectives are generated, self-directed learning is carried out and problem solving and critical evaluation skills are developed. Problems, often known as 'scenarios', are there not as things to be solved but as triggers for group discussion and the production of tasks and learning outcomes. Problems generate questions and it is the group's production of questions triggered by the scenario that activates the deep learning processes of PBL. In many ways PBL might more accurately be termed 'question based learning'.

PBL is an educational method that can be integrated with other learning modalities and can then contribute towards a major proportion of the learning on a module or degree course. PBL is ideally suited to degrees where there is a strong vocational element and a set of well-defined outcomes, often deriving from the prescriptions and standards required of professional bodies. Medicine was one of the first disciplines to develop PBL at Case Western Reserve University in the United States in the 1950s and McMaster University in Canada in the late 1960s, and its use in medical education is a model for many other areas which have adopted its method, such as dentistry, nursing, engineering, law, architecture, social work, management and economics.

HOW DOES A PBL CURRICULUM WORK?

Groups of about eight students meet with a facilitator two or three times a week to deal with a scenario, which could be a short description of a situation that the participants might encounter when they are professionally qualified. It could include a short video film. It will have been carefully worded by a curriculum team in such a way that at the first meeting, which normally lasts about an hour and a half, group members will be encouraged to ask questions leading to the generation of appropriate and relevant learning outcomes.

After the first session the group members next engage in about two or three days of work during which they have learning experiences and/or independent learning sessions where they learn material relevant to achieving the group's learning outcomes. At the next one-hour session, the information learned is presented and discussed by the group. An optional third session might be included where any final problems or questions generated in the preceding tutorial are resolved and where the group reflects on and evaluates its own working practices and progress.

A typical weekly timetable for a PBL course is shown in Table 5.1. Modules, courses or even whole degrees can be built up from a series of weekly scenarios designed to achieve the learning outcomes of the curriculum. The learning outcomes generated by the scenarios are designed to fit together to form an integrated and coherent learning structure that builds up knowledge, skills and attitudes in a graded and progressive way. In addition scenarios may be grouped together to form integrated sequences dealing with connected curriculum areas. In many forms of PBL there are specific themes running through the scenarios. For example in medical education each scenario could have a basic medical and clinical science theme, a community and population theme, a patient and doctor theme and a personal and professional development (PPD) theme. As will be outlined later, students are aware of these themes when dealing with the scenarios and conduct their analyses and formulate their questions with them in mind.

Note that the PBL sessions can be embedded in a structured week of timetabled sessions which might include a small number of core lectures, practical classes and work experience designed to complement the main themes of that week's scenario. It is in the provision of these additional learning sessions that considerable variation exists between different PBL programmes. The 'purest' form of PBL has just PBL tutorials and independent learning whereas other forms of PBL have increasing amounts of formal teaching including conventional lecturing. 'Pure' PBL is fairly rare and most courses include some formal teaching.

TABLE 5.1 A typical weekly PBL timetable in an undergraduate medical curriculum

	Monday	Tuesday	Wednesday	Thursday	Friday
Morning	3. **PBL tutorial** (Optional review of previous week) 1. **PBL tutorial** (New scenario)	■ Lectures ■ Seminars ■ Workshops ■ Demonstrations ■ Practical work Independent learning	Work experience	■ Lectures ■ Seminars ■ Workshops ■ Demonstrations ■ Practical work Independent learning	Personal and professional development 2. **PBL tutorial** (Presentation and discussion)
Afternoon	Independent learning	Independent learning	Free time	Independent learning	■ Lectures ■ Seminars ■ Workshops ■ Demonstrations ■ Practical work Independent learning

THE PBL TUTORIAL

The tutorial lies at the heart of PBL and exemplifies some of the most important aspects of SGT previously discussed in earlier chapters, for example the structure and organization of the session itself, the manipulation and monitoring of group dynamics and the skills of facilitation. The optimal group size for PBL is considered to be eight students and a facilitator. The students need to be trained to use PBL as does the facilitator (see later). The group meets in a suitably sized room provided with flip charts, white-boards and other appropriate resources, which might also include computers providing the scenarios and online learning materials. Over the years a specific sequence of events has crystallized out as being the best way to deal with the scenario although there are a number of variations. The Seven Step PBL process, described by Schmidt (1983), is described in the next section. Approximate timings are given for each section although these timings are variable depending on the group's stage and level of interest.

THE SEVEN STEP PBL PROCESS

- Step 1: Clarify terms and concepts
- Step 2: Define the problems
- Step 3: Analyse the problems – question, explain, hypothesize
- Step 4: Make a systematic list of the analysis
- Step 5: Formulate learning outcomes
- Step 6: Independent learning focused on learning outcomes
- Step 7: Synthesize and present new information.

One of the students is the chairperson, who has the responsibility for guiding the group through the steps; another student acts as a scribe, as there is frequently lots of writing to be recorded and processed. The role of the facilitator will be described in more detail later but he or she takes a back seat as far as possible and intervenes only to ensure that the group are on the right track and moving in the right direction. We will now go through the process and describing each step in turn, assuming a one-and-a-half-hour PBL tutorial session.

Step 1: Clarify terms and concepts

An example of a PBL scenario is given here:

> Ranjit Singh, 46, has just returned to England from the Indian subcontinent where he visited his brother and family for a period of one month. He lives with his wife, their four children and his parents in a three-bedroom terraced house in the Peartree district of Derby. Recently he has started coughing a lot, has little energy, is losing weight and has developed a fever. He visited his general practitioner (GP) after he coughed up some blood and developed chest pains.

The key question here is 'does everyone understand the scenario?' Are there any new technical terms that group members are not familiar with or phrases which are perhaps ambiguous and need clarification? Before continuing it is essential that the group knows precisely what the scenario means. This involves breaking down the scenario almost into its component words and phrases (and writing them on a flip chart) so that nothing is overlooked or taken for granted. This section may take only a few minutes to complete.

Step 2: Define the problems

Here the scenario has to be broken down into its component problems. Depending on the scenario there may be multiple problems embedded in the situation described. In addition the group may have to apply a thematic analysis to the problem. For example medicine themes might include basic medical science problems, clinical problems, community problems and personal and professional development problems. In the case of the scenario given here, some of the problems that might be produced by the group are:

- incidence of tuberculosis (TB) on the Indian subcontinent
- people living in overcrowded conditions
- the pathophysiology and microbiology of TB
- catching TB
- diagnosis of TB
- treatment of TB
- effects of TB on family and community
- dealing with sensitive cultural issues
- doctor's own immune status with respect to TB.

This phase might take ten to fifteen minutes.

Step 3: Analyse the problems – question, explain, hypothesize

The next phase is to take each problem in turn and subject it to a detailed analysis by using the combined knowledge and questioning power of the group. This phase is often carried out using a brainstorming technique and leads to the generation of many questions about each problem which are recorded by the scribe for later use. This is followed by attempts to provide answers and explanations in the form of suggestions or hypotheses, drawing on the background knowledge of the group. Here the scribe records key ideas, questions and possible answers on flip charts or white-boards around the room and a great deal of writing might take place. This process may take up to thirty minutes and is the largest element in the first tutorial.

In some forms of PBL at this stage additional information might be given to the group. For example in the scenario described above the results of particular clinical investigations might be introduced. This might have the effect of answering some of the questions that have been posed and even closing off some lines of inquiry or questioning.

Step 4: Make a systematic list of the analysis

The group will have now produced a list of questions, some of which will be unanswered, and some of which might have possible answers in the form of partial or incomplete explanations. In addition there might be some hypotheses or speculations that might require testing. The group now has to make a coherent list of this analysis bearing in mind any broad curriculum themes that need to be addressed. This might take fifteen minutes and again the scribe will be required to record the process.

Step 5: Formulate learning outcomes

The final process in this phase of the first tutorial is to attempt to turn the coherent list of questions, possible answers and hypotheses into a set of learning issues or outcomes that can form the basis of individual independent learning. Each student in the group needs to take away a set of learning outcomes that can guide his or her own self-study. This might take about fifteen minutes.

In the case of the scenario described, Table 5.2 gives a brief list of learning outcomes that might have been generated via the five PBL steps described.

■ **TABLE 5.2** Possible learning outcomes created by an undergraduate medical PBL group after dealing with a scenario

---

Basic and clinical sciences
- Describe mechanisms and common causes of cough.
- Describe types of clinical investigations available for patients with cough.
- Interpret a chest X-ray.
- Outline the microbiology of mycobacterium tuberculosis.
- Describe the immune response to TB, its use in diagnosis and the tuberculin test.
- Describe clinical and pathological manifestations of TB.
- Outline the drug regimes for treating TB, their mode of action, side-effects and the problem of drug resistance.

Community and population
- Describe the epidemiology of TB and the impact of socio-economic factors.
- Discuss the social and family issues associated with TB in the community.

Patient and doctor
- Describe how communication problems can be dealt with in ethnic minorities.
- Describe the perception of TB in Asian communities and the problem of stigmatization.
- Deal with issues of confidentiality versus compulsory notification in issues concerning patient autonomy.
- Describe how to ensure compliance with complex and long-term drug regimes.
- Persuade family members to be immunized.

Personal and professional development
- Doctor as patient: awareness of personal immune status.

Step 6: Independent learning focused on learning outcomes

The longest step in the PBL process is where students go to consult resources in libraries, web sites and a variety of other teaching and learning resources to find answers to their questions, to test their hypotheses and to achieve their learning outcomes. In most versions of PBL each student attempts all the learning outcomes rather than a specific set, although this can be varied. Students may attend conventional lectures, practical classes or seminars and even have individual tutorials with teachers. They can engage in work experience which might, in the case of medical, nursing or dental students, for example, take the form of short clinical attachments in outpatient clinics, operating theatres, hospital wards or general practices. All of these additional learning experiences should complement their independent learning activities and contribute towards the generation of a coherent and comprehensive response to the learning outcomes, which will be presented to the group in the next PBL tutorial.

Step 7: Synthesize and present new information

At the next PBL tutorial conventionally both the chairperson and scribe are replaced by new group members. A variety of presentation and discussion techniques can be used to enable students to present their findings to the rest of the group. For example, each group member could be asked to present a brief summary of their findings using an OHP or else individuals could be asked to present on specific learning outcomes. The facilitator ensures that all the objectives have been covered as far as possible.

Sometimes, inevitably, this final session might agree that certain questions have not been adequately answered or could even generate some additional questions. In this case a final brief session can be held to deal with these outstanding issues. In this session it is also useful for the facilitator to review and summarize the key issues that have been covered and to get the group to evaluate their working practices and engage in some reflection. This is where metacognition occurs as learners deepen their insight into how they learn. This can lead to the development of positive attitudes to learning that serve as a foundation for lifelong learning and continuing professional development.

THE EDUCATIONAL RATIONALE FOR PBL

> The most powerful learning occurs when the student is dealing with uncertainty.
>
> (John Dewey 1938: 32)

Now that PBL has been described and the PBL process explained, you can more easily make comparisons with other forms of SGT and begin to understand the educational reasons why it is considered to be one of the most powerful methods of learning. As described in Chapter 1, the benefits of SGT derive from a combination of content and process and there can be no better fusion of these two elements than PBL. Participants not only develop a deep-level understanding of the content but also develop a range of communication and professional skills allied to a positive attitude towards learning. PBL is therefore a highly integrated system of education in which cognitive content, professional context and interpersonal processes are intertwined. The evidence for its effectiveness will be reviewed later.

Activities and learning processes occurring during PBL

In broad terms PBL involves active, collaborative, student-centred learning, coupled to highly motivated independent learning. Learning is reinforced by talking, doing and presenting. It is worthwhile listing some of the key activities and processes that students can engage in when conducting PBL to demonstrate how it provides such a wide-ranging set of learning opportunities:

- thinking: analysing, synthesizing, critically evaluating, problem solving
- activating, evaluating and using prior knowledge
- communicating: talking, discussing, arguing, empathizing, listening
- questioning and challenging
- imagining, suggesting, hypothesizing
- collaborating, co-operating and sharing
- taking responsibility
- self-monitoring and reflecting
- searching for information
- processing, summarizing and recording information
- presenting.

The use of scenarios that have been structured around actual problems and situations faced by practitioners has a profound effect on the learning process. By using scenarios and the associated problems and questions generated from their analysis learning immediately becomes professionally contextualized and relevant; it has high face validity. Students automatically have to activate their prior knowledge in order to start thinking about the problem confronting them. This has been shown to enhance learning (Norman and Schmidt 1992). In addition they find themselves in a state of uncertainty, described as 'cognitive dissonance' (Festinger 1957) where their existing knowledge base and mental framework is challenged either by the problem itself or by the knowledge and experience of other group members. Such a state motivates the learner to seek mental equilibrium by finding the answer to questions during self-directed learning. By learning in collaborative groups not only are communication skills developed and personal insights into strengths and weaknesses gained, but participants become highly motivated to achieve their learning objectives because of group dynamics and positive peer pressure.

Brookfield (1987) has reviewed concepts from cognitive psychology and theories of adult learning that also underpin PBL:

- learners know what they might gain from the effort of learning
- learners determine the course and pace of their learning
- learners perceive that learning is related to their own experience
- the topics used are those which help them deal more effectively with their everyday problems
- topics relate to actual tasks and problems
- learning is seen to enhance job satisfaction and self-esteem
- learning incorporates elements of challenge to promote critical analysis
- learning takes account of the needs of the organization and society as well as development of the individual.

PBL has also been described as an example of 'contextual learning' (Coles 1991) where learning takes place in an appropriate and relevant context and students elaborate their knowledge by seeing the interrelationships between different areas of knowledge. Furthermore, the elaboration of knowledge during learning has been shown to enhance retrieval (Norman and Schmidt 1992). PBL can also be seen as a response to the acquisition of professional expertise. Traditional learning is often dominated by the acquisition of content in the form of propositional knowledge or 'knowledge that'. However, professional expertise in addition requires the acquisition of procedural knowledge or 'knowing how'. Savin-Baden (2000) has shown that PBL, which encourages the integration of these two types of knowledge, leads to a greater insight into multidimensional problems.

Professional attitudes towards learning

Schön's concept of the 'reflective practitioner' (Schön 1983) also includes the integration of propositional and procedural knowledge. Schön argued that traditional education emphasized 'technical rationality' where learning was focused on abstract and stylized situations divorced from reality and dominated by propositional knowledge. However, when learners began to practise in real situations they found themselves in the 'swampy lowlands' where they began to acquire procedural knowledge in a complex and frequently indeterminate environment filled with values and emotions. Here they found that knowledge ('knowing-in-action') was often tacit and not necessarily based on empirical or rational evidence. PBL can lead to the development of professional attitudes towards knowledge, learning which can help learners cope with this transition to professionalism and professional practice. Reflective students, encouraged to think about how they learn (the process of metacognition), realize that knowledge is not just given but is actively constructed. Furthermore, they see that the process of acquiring and elaborating deep-level understanding is facilitated by the interplay between individuals in group discussion. Crucially they also recognize that they have the ultimate responsibility for filling the gaps and weaknesses in their own mental models by questioning and independent learning. Such realizations are more likely to generate lifelong learners and reflective practitioners who will engage in continuing professional development.

ADULT LEARNING

PBL also fulfils many of the characteristics of adult learning as shown in the following examples of conditions for effective adult learning:

- Active learning through posing own questions and seeking the respective answers.
- Integrated learning, learning in a variety of subjects or disciplines concurrently through learning in the context in which the learning is to be applied in real-life situations.
- Cumulative learning to achieve growing familiarity through a sequence of learning experiences that are relevant to the student's goals, experiences that become progressively less straightforward but more complex, as well as less non-threatening but progressively more challenging.

■ Learning for understanding, rather than for recall of isolated facts through appropriate opportunities to reflect on their educational experiences, and through frequent feedback, linked with opportunities to practise the application of what has been learned.

(adapted from Engel 1991: 25)

THE PBL FACILITATOR

One of the aims of PBL is to encourage the students to manage the process as far as possible. However, the facilitator plays a pivotal role in the proceedings to such an extent that without appropriate and sensitive interventions, the PBL session could go off track. In keeping with the student-centred nature of PBL, the facilitator should let the students be responsible for their own learning and has to let the students do most of the work. However, the facilitator must monitor the activity and progress of the group and may provide help in the form of suggestions. The facilitator is part of the faculty PBL team and as such will know the overall direction the group should be taking and the objectives they should be heading towards. They may also, in some versions of PBL, have additional material they can feed to the group at appropriate moments. The facilitator can intervene to subtly steer the group in a particular direction or to encourage them to ask questions in an important area they might have missed. However, in general the facilitator is not there to either provide or answer questions concerning the content of the scenario. This can be a difficult activity to engage in and PBL facilitators require training and continuing support to ensure their role helps the group to function optimally.

As mentioned in Chapter 3, facilitators of SGT sessions must have an appropriate and relevant attitude towards teaching and learning. This is even more important in PBL facilitation. In particular facilitators must put their desire to tell students information on hold and they must trust the students to do the work. Facilitators also work in close proximity to group members for two or three hours a week which will inevitably lead to the development of more complex teacher–student relationships. Rogers (1983) has stressed that teaching is essentially a relationship and PBL facilitators need to be particularly aware of this and to acknowledge and reflect on its effects on themselves. PBL facilitators become partners in the learning process. They get to know students' strengths and weaknesses and they should be concerned for the individual development of each student in the group. Facilitators have to be prepared to expose their own ignorance and be prepared to say 'I don't know'. In PBL the boundaries between the academic, the personal and the pastoral become blurred and facilitators need to steer a path between the roles of teacher, parent, consultant, mediator, counsellor, confidant and learner.

SETTING UP A PBL COURSE

Schools that have made the decision to move over to a PBL curriculum often take two or three years before the system is ready to implement. PBL is a significant change in the teaching and learning ethos and staff need plenty of time for consultation and training. Even when a PBL school has been created from scratch with newly appointed staff, the process will take at least two years. A curriculum has to be defined and then scenarios and problems carefully constructed that will lead students to acquire the desired learning outcomes. Staff need to be trained to become PBL facilitators and newly arrived students also need to be inducted into the PBL process.

Attempting to achieve the same learning outcomes by having a PBL curriculum running alongside a conventionally delivered curriculum can cause problems affecting both systems. Either the PBL students envy the 'spoon-fed' conventional students or else the conventional students envy the 'fun' and freedom the PBL students have. The ethos of the two systems is so radically different that it might be wise for the sanity of both staff and students to keep them apart.

EVIDENCE FOR THE EFFECTIVENESS OF PBL

The trouble with PBL is that you have to learn a whole bunch of stuff that you won't need until after you graduate.

(A PBL student)

PBL is now used in hundreds of higher academic schools worldwide and has been endorsed by many professional medical and health science bodies such as the Association of American Medical Colleges, the World Federation of Medical Education (Walton and Matthews 1989), the World Health Organization (WHO 1993), the World Bank (1993) and the English National Board for Nursing, Midwifery and Health Visiting (English National Board (ENB) 1998). Nevertheless PBL is such a radically different way of learning that it frequently provokes sceptical questioning in people coming across it for the first time and it is always having to justify its existence and demonstrate its effectiveness. In that respect it is one of the most heavily researched areas of higher education; since the early 1990s a number of large studies have been carried out and meta-analyses reported (Albanese and Mitchell 1993; Berkson 1993; Vernon and Blake 1993; Wilkie 2000; Newman 2003). However, it is important to recognize that there are a wide variety of PBL types and easy comparisons are not always possible; Barrows (1986) differentiated six types of PBL whereas Savin-Baden (2000) identified five.

Overall Vernon and Blake (1993) concluded that the PBL approach was superior to more traditional methods. Albanese and Mitchell (1993), in reviewing twenty years of literature, argued that PBL was more enjoyable and that PBL graduates performed as well and sometimes better on clinical examinations and faculty evaluations. In addition PBL graduates had better communication skills and were more likely to engage in continuing professional development opportunities. However, PBL students in a few instances scored lower on basic knowledge tests and felt they were less well prepared. In addition some problems in clinical reasoning were identified. On the other hand Berkson (1993) asserted that PBL graduates were indistinguishable from their traditional counterparts but agreed with Albanese and Mitchell (1993) that PBL was more costly when used to teach over one hundred students.

The problem of basic knowledge gaps and the potential for PBL students to have incorrect knowledge is an important issue. The question is: does it matter? The fact that students taught via conventional means do not all score 100 per cent in examinations indicates that they too have knowledge gaps. Also the fact that teachers have stood up and covered the curriculum in traditional lectures is no guarantee that students will learn all the material. In addition there is evidence that significant amounts of basic knowledge, taught in medical courses, are not required for clinical practice and are perceived as irrelevant by practitioners (Clack 1994).

In PBL what is more important than trying to achieve an essentially unachievable complete factual knowledge is to develop the student's attitude towards learning and their evaluation of their own strengths and weaknesses. Learners need to be encouraged to be honest with each other, to challenge each other's knowledge and to admit when they are wrong or don't know the answer. Students need to be made aware of the iterative nature of knowledge, that facts are approached on many occasions from different directions and in different contexts. The idea that facts are acquired and memorized once is unrealistic.

EXAMPLES FROM DIFFERENT DISCIPLINES

Here are a few PBL scenarios from various disciplines.

Nursing

Mrs Sandhu, a 40-year-old Sikh woman is admitted to your ward. She was diagnosed with breast cancer eighteen months ago and has since developed liver and bone metastases. She is very thin, dehydrated, in a lot of pain and crying. She is accompanied by her sister and eldest daughter Sandeep, 12. Her husband is at home looking after their other 5-year-old daughter.

Electrical engineering

The university has decided to host a swimming competition for local schools in the university's new swimming pool complex. Rather than pay for outside contractors to supply the timing equipment, staff in the Electrical Engineering Department have volunteered to build a system themselves, supervising final year students to design, construct and install the equipment.

International politics

Boldova was a semi-autonomous province within Meningia, a grouping of old European states held together in the Soviet bloc after the Second World War. Since the collapse of the Soviet Union and its replacement by the Russian Federation, Meningia has forced Boldova's largely Muslim majority into exile in neighbouring Kamania, causing a major humanitarian crisis in the region. The houses and the jobs of the Boldovans have been given to ethnic Meningians, who are Orthodox Christians, any remaining Muslims have been persecuted and even murdered by Meningian 'special forces' and many mosques have been destroyed. The president of Meningia, Harradin Silovic, a former psychiatrist, has declared that all the Orthodox Christians in the neighbouring states must be incorporated into 'Greater Meningia', fulfilling the promise made to all ethnic

Meningians after the battle of Blatto in 1497. This implies the annexation and 'ethnic cleansing' of Kamania. Meningia has repeatedly ignored United Nations resolutions to stop ethnic cleansing and has prevented relief agencies from sending in aid to Boldovan refugee camps. The government of Kamania is threatening to invade Boldova to push back Meningian forces who are massing on the border. NATO is meeting in Brussels to decide what move it should make to restore European stability.

Social work

Police have been called, by neighbours, to the house of Mr White, an unemployed 30-year-old labourer who lives with his partner and her three children from another relationship, Donna 3, Kylie 5 and Wayne 11. Mr White, who is a heavy cannabis user and has been treated for depression, has a history of violent conduct towards his partner, who has had to stay in a women's refuge on a number of occasions. The eldest boy, Wayne, has recently been caught by the police for breaking into parked cars. All three children have been looked after by foster parents in the past. On this occasion Mr White has assaulted his partner so severely that she has been taken to hospital with a suspected fractured skull. The police have arrested Mr White and are considering if he needs to be sectioned under the Mental Health Act. A policewoman is minding the children until a social worker arrives.

Economics

Van Tran, a 15-year-old Vietnamese boy, works in a factory manufacturing trainers for export to the United States. He works nine hours a day, six days a week, earning $12, which is almost twice the average wage. On a number of occasions his hands have been injured but his manager has bandaged him up and sent him back to work. His father thinks he is well paid and hopes his job can continue as it helps support their family. He is concerned about rumours that the factory might close because there is a movement to boycott the trainers in the USA.

📖 FURTHER READING

Boud, D. and Feletti, G. (1997) *The Challenge of Problem Based Learning*, 2nd edn, London: Kogan Page.

Savin-Baden, M. (2000) *Problem-based Learning in Higher Education: Untold Stories*, Buckingham: Society for Research in Higher Education and Open University Press.

Wilkie, K. (2000) 'The nature of problem-based learning', in S. Glen and K. Wilkie (eds) *Problem-based Learning in Nursing*, London: Macmillan Press.

USEFUL WEB SITES

http://www.hss.coventry.ac.uk/pbl/index.htm The UK PBL web site is hosted by Coventry University and supported by the LTSN Generic Centre. The aim of the web site is to provide up to date and innovative trigger materials together with information about where problem-based learning is being used in the UK (accessed 19 October 2003).

http://interact.bton.ac.uk/pbl/ The University of Brighton has set up a PBL Directory that already contains details of PBL courses currently running in more than 20 countries (accessed 19 October 2003).

http://www.udel.edu/pbl/others.html The University of Delaware's PBL site carries information about related web links, PBL conferences and discussion lists (accessed 19 October 2003).

http://www.art.man.ac.uk/ENGLISH/PROJECTS/pbl.htm The University of Manchester's Department of English and American Studies PBL Project page (accessed 19 October 2003).

http://www.hebes.mdx.ac.uk/teaching/Research/PEPBL/index.htm The University of Middlesex hosts the PEPBL web site. PEPBL is a three year research project that started in March 2000 designed to evaluate the effectiveness of PBL courses by looking at two post-registration nursing programmes.

Chapter 6

Student-led seminars and tutor-less tutorials

WHY ASK STUDENTS TO TAKE THE LEAD?

There are a number of reasons for wishing to adopt student-centred and collaborative learning approaches in SGT; some are pragmatic while others arise from educational principle and the need to support the development of professional skills and encourage lifelong learning.

Although student numbers have increased, resources and funding haven't to the same extent, so the benefits of encouraging and supporting students to learn from and with each other are obvious. It is also clear that higher education should aim to equip students with the abilities to update and continue to learn independently after graduation. In the main this will happen through the help and guidance provided informally by friends and colleagues rather than by attending formal courses and training events (Boud *et al.* 2001). So student-led and peer tutoring approaches do support the development of collaborative learning skills and the future needs of students.

There is also evidence that co-operative learning can lead to improvements in student learning and achievement. Johnson and Johnson (1985) considered the results from more than a hundred research studies of co-operative learning and concluded that there were several features that could be generally considered to improve the performance and attainment of students. These include

- high-quality reasoning strategies
- constructive management of conflict
- more elaborate information processing
- greater peer regulation and encouragement of efforts to achieve

- more active mutual involvement in learning
- beneficial interaction between students of different achievement levels
- feelings of support and psychological acceptance
- more positive attitudes towards subject areas
- greater perceptions of fairness of grading.

Falchikov (2001) also describes the positive effects of collaborative e-learning in terms of the increase in self-esteem, motivation, attendance, completion rates and liking of the topic and the institution experienced by students.

However, there is also evidence from the research that within the peer-tutoring relationship the tutor gains more than the tutee (Bargh and Schul 1980; Annis 1983). So the idea that 'If you really want to understand something, try and teach it' seems to be borne out. Later in this chapter ways of spreading the benefit to the peer-tutees or the non-presenting students will be considered.

In this chapter we explore the use of student-centred learning in the SGT setting. This comprises a spectrum of approaches that includes at one end the tutored seminar programme in which students are asked to prepare and present the topics for class discussion. These student presentations result in the classes often being referred to (a little confusingly) as *student-led seminars*.

Moving along the continuum are SGT sessions in which the tutor is completely absent but he or she has provided the framework, structure, focus (and resources?) to support useful collaborative work. These sessions may be called *tutor-less tutorials, student learning sets, base groups, peer learning teams* and so on.

At the far end of the continuum are student-organized and led small groups in which the students have been asked to, or have spontaneously decided to, formalize their collaborative learning with little or no direction from the tutor. Such groups may be referred to as *study groups* or *student support groups*. Figure 6.1 aims to illustrate this balance of control and leadership across the range of SGT approaches that can be adopted in support of student-centred learning.

PROCTORIALS

When the students within a learning group are drawn from different levels of the course and the more experienced students have the specific

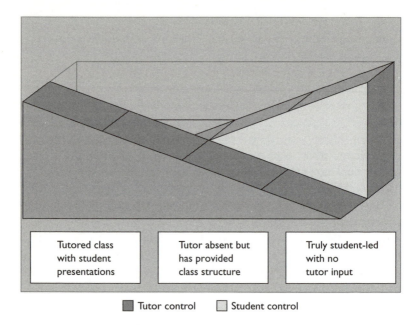

| Tutored class with student presentations | Tutor absent but has provided class structure | Truly student-led with no tutor input |

■ Tutor control   □ Student control

FIGURE 6.1 The control continuum in SGT approaches

role of tutoring or supporting their less experienced peers, then the groupings may be referred to as proctorials and the student tutors called proctors or peer Mentors. A related approach known as supplemental instruction (SI) invites second-year volunteer students to guide first-year students and help them learn from their lectures and classes in one-hour weekly sessions. As SI systems typically operate in content heavy and intensive courses, such as in medicine and engineering, the SI leaders do not introduce new material but work to help first-year students make sense and 'construct' their own understanding of material already delivered in lectures. Second-year volunteers are trained in group dynamics and study strategies for their role. SI is reported to improve student performance, develop a range of study skills and cognitive skills as well as reducing dropout rates. For more information please have a look at the SI home page and linked resources – details are given in the further reading at the end of this chapter.

STUDENT PRESENTATIONS AND STUDENT-LED SEMINARS

One of the most common approaches used in seminar classes is to ask a student, a pair of students or a small group of students to prepare a short (five to fifteen minutes) presentation on assigned readings or a discussion topic for the class. The students may have limited choice in the topics that they prepare and usually know their assignments well in advance. In some courses seminar lists and topic allocations are given out at the beginning of the semester or term. A standard approach is that the student or students give their presentation and this is then followed by a full group discussion of the key issues raised. Often the tutor provides the focus for this discussion by asking one or more questions about the presentation. A slight variation on this method is to ask the class to work in small groups of four or five to discuss a particular question or questions arising from the initial student presentations before feeding back their responses to the whole class.

The tutor may choose to ask questions that are designed to simply check that the non-presenting students have followed and understood the presentation; however, the questions can have a more ambitious purpose such as:

■ to help fill the gaps in the topic not covered by the presentation
■ to correct any errors and misinterpretations given in the talk
■ to extend, extrapolate and deepen thinking on key topics raised by the presenters
■ to raise alternative approaches or different interpretations for comparison with those presented.

By using small group, follow-up discussions in this way the tutor can minimize one of the noted difficulties associated with traditional student-led seminars. This is that the students who are leading the seminar are very involved in the class and have prepared well (usually!) but that the non-presenting students may abdicate their responsibilities, attend passively and behave like an audience rather than as participants.

ENCOURAGING ALL TO PREPARE FOR THE STUDENT-LED SEMINAR

Some tutors ask all the students in the class to prepare as if they were going to lead the tutorial and at the start of the class, select two students at random to actually do so. In this case all the students will have undertaken a basic level of preparation for all their classes rather than preparing in depth for some. For example, all the students could be directed to do the designated reading, come up with half a dozen questions about it and prepare a very brief summary of key findings or issues.

An alternative strategy is that the seminar leaders, selected in advance, are asked to prepare in depth and in detail while the non-presenting students negotiate to undertake a reduced and more superficial level of preparation, e.g. read the core article or chapters only. So the students have 'heavy' and 'lighter' weeks during the course. Decisions about approach are usually based on the overall workload of the students during their studies and the attitudes and preferences of the academic module leaders.

INVOLVING THE NON-PRESENTERS

For the tutor who wishes to encourage greater participation of all students during the class, there are several teaching and learning strategies available. You may wish to give this guidance to your student presenters?

Leading seminars and discussions

Student pairs

Pairs of students lead the seminar, one as the presenter and one as the facilitator (it being the facilitator's job to involve their peers in discussing the topic presented). With guidance from the tutor the pair need to prepare the seminar together (this may not always be possible to do face-to-face, but can be done virtually using email or discussion boards). In their planning they need to think about how they are going to reach out to their peers and involve them in further debate, analysis and evaluation. (You could ask your students to read the following section to help them with this role and task?)

Debates

A debate may be possible. There may be polar points of view, two theories, solutions or ideologies that can be argued, two historical or political interpretations, two experimental models or mathematical methods that can be compared and contrasted. If the topic presented lends itself to a debate fun can be had. The non-presenting students may be given a viewpoint or a stance to defend or support before the presentation to enable them to begin thinking about their arguments and evidence. The presenters may wish to provide additional articles or resources to help this process. After the presentation the students can work together in two groups to develop their cases. The final section of the seminar is the debate itself in which both sides put forward their points of view. The tutor may take the role of the chairperson who manages the discussion or the arbitrator who eases negotiation. If appropriate the tutor may cast the vote deciding which side has won the argument that day, or the students can decide that for themselves. This decision could happen during the tutorial or as a follow-up exchange on the class discussion board or via an email discussion list. There are many variations on the debate theme and it is an approach that, with a little thought, can lend itself to both qualitative and quantitative disciplines.

Using questions to focus discussions

Divide the class into groups of two, three or four and give the groups a question or, better still, a number of questions to consider. After giving the groups enough working time you can then ask each group to respond to one of the questions in turn. You could ask a spokesperson from the group to explain their group's answer or, for a change and to speed things up, you could write the question clearly on the top of an overhead acetate and ask the students to write their agreed answer below.

Using triggers for discussion

You can give students a newspaper clipping and ask them to think about it and then tell the class what it is about and why it is interesting, important, relevant etc. A variety of stimuli can be used in this way from journal articles, artifacts, poems, demonstrations, a piece of music, a short video clip and so on.

Using personal stories, vignettes and case studies

Following an introductory presentation to explain the situation and context (historically, politically, sociologically, scientifically, medically or whatever) the students could be given personal accounts that show a range of experiences or viewpoints to illustrate learning points. The stories can be drawn from autobiographies, fiction, the Internet, research, published case studies as well as from personal experience. The inputs can be a mix of truth and fiction, or you can amend the true ones in order to anonymize them or make them more relevant to the class. The stories can be used in the seminar in a number of different ways by setting different tasks or questions for the students to work on, for example, 'What would you do here?', 'What are the options?', 'What do you think happened next?', 'Why did that happen . . . ?'

Using a quiz

A quiz can be used as a warm-up activity to remind the students of the content of previously held discussions and help them to refocus on today's topic. Students often enjoy quizzes as they feel less daunting than a 'test' and yet can serve a similar purpose.

There are various kinds of quizzes:

- The questions are given out, each student writes something down, then answers are read out and the students swap their answer sheets and mark each other's.
- The questions are read out, and groups of students agree answers and jointly write them down before groups swap answer sheets and mark each other's.
- The questions are asked and the teams reply verbally, often through a team spokesperson who answers on behalf of their team, maybe gaining points for correct answers and losing points for incorrect answers, then offering the question to another team. Such an approach would be 'higher energy' and would need to be closely managed to ensure that learning was taking place.
- Questions could be provided on a quiz sheet with true/false options or using a multiple choice format. The sheets could be used by individuals or by groups.

 100

Alternatively the whole class could be organized around a set of quiz questions. Students, working in groups, could be asked to work collaboratively to answer them. Then responses could be discussed within the class. Using this format allows questions to be asked that have a range of different possible answers rather than needing to be so clearly 'right' or 'wrong'.

Study groups

The tutor usually sets up 'study groups' as an integral part of a course, in order to provide a forum for course-related issues to be addressed. Indeed membership of a study group may well be a requirement of the course and the tutor is likely to assign individuals to specific study groups in order to provide equity and encourage a cross-sectional mix of constituents in each group in terms of background, experience, gender, culture and so on (see Figure 6.2).

Subsequently group meetings are organized by the students themselves in a semi-autonomous fashion. The tutor may provide guidance to the students on how they can do this and may suggest co-operative tasks that can involve the whole group. The tutor should also keep in regular contact with the group to both monitor and motivate, although this can be done at a distance using email for example.

FIGURE 6.2 A study group

Although students list the personal benefits, such as gaining support, confidence building, sharing ideas, as the main values associated with being a member of a study group, there can be significant academic gains too. Study groups can provide a forum in which students are able to explore their discipline in a relaxed and supportive environment and are therefore more likely to 'take risks' and discuss issues and concepts in greater depth. Students may also develop professional skills such as how to run and organize a group meeting, how to minute and record decisions and outcomes and how to learn to work together across cultural, linguistic, gender divides etc.

It can help maintain the cohesion of a study group if members can share a common goal and if the members can work together towards the completion of a joint task or activity. This could be the preparation of a joint report, giving a group presentation or the production of their study group web page.

Setting up a study group for your course: some advice

- Keep the groups quite small (between five and eight students).
- Particularly in the early days, give the group specific tasks to complete co-operatively in order to give the group a focus and a purpose for being.
- Provide guidance on where and how often the group is expected to meet.
- Provide guidance on how they can develop ground rules to work together.
- Monitor the groups by requesting that they keep minutes and nominate a group liaison person whom you can easily communicate with and through.
- If possible, build in an assessment component that rewards students for playing an active role in the study group and encourages their reflection on that contribution, e.g. a learning log or diary that includes critical incidents and associated reflective commentaries.

LEARNING EXCHANGES

You scratch my back and I'll play ball with you.

A group of students can work together in order to investigate and research a wider range of topics by taking one aspect each and then seeking to teach their peers about their allocated topic – with their colleagues reciprocating in kind.

The exchange can happen relatively informally and privately within a collaborating group or it can become much more of an event and mimic a mini-conference (Sampson and Cohen 2001). The students can be asked to share their findings formally, using both an oral presentation and by providing copies of a brief, written report for each other. Alternatively the exchange could happen virtually, with the students being asked to post their written reports to online discussion forums using virtual learning environments (VLEs) such as Blackboard or WebCT pages. The group can then use the discussion boards to give and receive feedback and ask and respond to each other's questions. (For further discussion of VLEs, please refer to Chapter 8.)

Support groups can also be established to formalize reciprocal peer feedback. Students can help each other to develop their 'written assignment skills' and by so doing develop their interpersonal and communication skills. A process of prescribed *dialogue* can be used within the support group – for example, for each written assignment students are asked to work in a group of three and they should meet together three times:

- *Meeting 1:* Week 1 – work with the title to discuss initial plans and to help the writers to clearly focus.
- *Meeting 2:* Week 3 – after writing the first draft, meet to discuss to what extent the draft has achieved what was intended and to talk through any problems or issues the writers have had.
- *Meeting 3:* After the assignment has been marked, meet with the support group to clarify what has been achieved, what has been learnt and what this means for future assignments.

The students can usefully keep a learning journal in which they record their thoughts on how the process of group dialogue has supported them in developing skills and writing their assignments. Such a journal would also provide invaluable feedback on the approach for staff. For more on this approach developed by Dr Arlene Gilpin and colleagues please see http://www.escalate.ac.uk/exchange

103

EXAMPLES FROM DIFFERENT DISCIPLINES

Student-led seminars in drama

What is a student-led seminar? The student-led seminar is not a teaching slot but a space for student discussion and debate, for the exchange and testing of ideas. This space is yours to discuss ideas, problems and issues in relation to television. After the first seminar, discussion will not be led by the tutor but by a small group of students.

How will the groups be formed? In the first seminar of the module we will sort you into small groups. These groups will work together on researching and organizing an assessed student-led seminar, so you need to think about not only who you might get on with, but also how easily you can contact the other members.

What will the groups have to do? The group leading the seminar will take responsibility for the seminar. This will involve researching a topic, setting the agenda for the seminar discussion of that topic, planning the format of the seminar, and running it on the day.

Your task in leading the seminar is not to produce a polished public presentation nor to read out a paper, but to do the preliminary preparatory work necessary to define issues and questions for the whole seminar to address.

How will the groups go about this? It will be the task of the students leading the seminar to meet several times before the seminar in order to

- share out tasks – for example reading can be shared out, photocopies made, viewing shared out
- pool ideas and decide on the agenda for discussion and the format of the seminar
- decide how to organize the seminar on the day, how to initiate any pre-discussion activities, and how best to chair the whole group discussion.

How will the group in charge of the seminar lead the discussion? The group leading the class will initially introduce the seminar. To begin with, responses and interventions from the rest of the group may be addressed to the students who are chairing. If the tutor is present and particularly if sitting in a prominent position, there may be a tendency for seminar members to address their comments to the tutor. If, however, the discussion is to belong to the whole group, it is important to prevent the tutor slipping back into a teaching role and commenting on everything that is said. The trick in leading discussions is to gradually draw in other members of the group so that people can talk across the group to each other rather than through the chairperson. Nevertheless, if discussion gets heated, and it is obvious that someone is trying, unsuccessfully, to be heard, your role as discussion leaders is to make a space for that person.

How do you get discussion started? There are various ways you can organize the whole group seminar and you will need to give some thought to your strategy, for example:

- opening brainstorm (writing down as many ideas as come to mind) on key images, or questions with the whole group on the whiteboard
- dividing the seminar into small groups to discuss your questions, video extracts or critical quotations, as a warm-up
- presenting two opposed views on a particular issue, setting up a debate into which the whole group can enter
- putting forward key ideas, issues and so on, selected by yourselves.

You may want to start in small groups and join one or more of the groups to join discussions. You may want to present ideas or information that are important to the agenda you are setting, or have strong opinions you want to share with the group, but you must find ways of doing this in a few minutes. You may find it timesaving to photocopy collective or individual 'position' statements or relevant quotations for the whole group. You may want to use a video extract in which case make sure you cue the video before the seminar (and have clips on standard rather than long play). You may want to write up questions on the white-board, in which case arrive early for the seminar. (This material was adapted from guidance given to students at http://mcs.staffs.ac.uk/modulesppt/btvdrama/tvdrama.htm, accessed 9 June 2003.)

Advocating student-led tutorials in law

Resources for teaching decrease, but demands of learning increase. How can we provide students with a richer educational experience with reduced resources? With fewer resources available to support small group tutorials, their frequency reduces or their size increases. Either way their potential value for individual students is diminished. Responding to this crisis, but also trying to find opportunities for students to extend their interpersonal and transferable skills, student-led tutorials (SLTs) were introduced to the Law Faculty's criminal law course in 1996–7. Each tutorial group was encouraged to meet before its tutor-led tutorial (TLT), with their detailed worksheets. They appointed a chairperson, distributed prime responsibility for the next tutorial's work and then shared and discussed their preparation for the forthcoming tutor-led class. About half the SLTs stopped meeting before the end of the course, although those who maintained them found them very valuable. A problem was that the students did not have a model of what a successful SLT looked like and could not immediately appreciate all the additional benefits, in terms of transferable skills, that they developed, particularly when chairing. So the Teaching Support and Media Studies (TSMS) Video Unit at the University of Southampton has produced a video, with support materials. This shows some law students meeting in a SLT and then in the corresponding TLT. Working on problems, provided by the tutor, they think, argue, discuss with and learn from each other. They work together delegating, supporting, encouraging, putting peer pressure on those slipping or not being co-operative. They gain valuable experience, and skills, in chairing, etc. As a careers adviser and employer comment in the video, the skills and experiences sought by interviewers will be gained and honed in SLTs. The video is being used to give students a model of what SLTs are, how they work and why they are so valuable. As both students and tutors comment, in the video, SLTs provide a rich experience that enables the TLT to be much more effective and efficient, while the students, in the video, discuss a criminal law problem that would not inhibit the programme being of value to any other discipline that uses small-group teaching (see http://www.clt.soton.ac.uk/tldg/proj9798.htm, accessed 9 June 2003).

Proctoring in philosophy

A tutor group of about twelve first-year students attend a proctorial at the beginning of each week of the taught course. The proctorials are led by third-year 'proctors'. The purpose of these sessions is to provide additional structured guidance for first-year students. During the proctorial the students are encouraged to work through a series of questions relating to recent lectures. The students then take this preparatory thinking, responses and questions onto a tutored tutorial that runs at the end of the week. The proctors can gain credit for their input by registering for a third-year optional module 'Proctoring' that is assessed through a written exam. The exam asks proctors to give responses to between three and six generalized question scenarios drawing upon their experiences of proctoring and reflecting upon their role specification and the training they received. (This section is reporting the work of Hayler and Funnel (1998) at the University of Leeds.)

Presentations in statistics

Of all the teaching strategies that I explored, the small group presentations were, in fact, the most successful. The strategy here was to supply each small group with either the same set of data and different tasks (in which case a full investigation of the data could be undertaken), or to give each small group a different set of data and the same task. Each group of students then worked through the data and was given a 5-minute slot at the end of the session to report back to the wider group on their mini-project, the techniques they used and what they had found.

(Bramley 1996: 75)

 A cautionary tale!

I certainly don't like it if you get tutorials where the guy just comes along and sits down and makes you stand up and do the work on the blackboard. Usually he picks on people that can't do it, which I think is terrible because you get stuck up at the blackboard and made to look a fool and it switches you right off . . . I think I'm not going to do that if this guy's going to do that to me, because it takes you so long to do the question; and it makes you very unhappy with that particular course, so I lose interest in the course.

(Student taking physics, reported in Ramsden 1984: 198)

FURTHER READING

Boud, D., Cohen, R. and Sampson, J. (2001) *Peer Learning in Higher Education: Learning from and with each other*, London: Kogan Page.

Falchikov, N. (2001) *Learning Together: Peer Tutoring in Higher Education*, London: Routledge/Falmer.

Slavin, R., Sharon, S., Kagan, S., Hertz-Lazarowitz, R., Webb, C. and Schmuck, R. (eds) (1985) *Learning to Cooperate, Cooperation to Learn*, New York and London: Plenum Press.

USEFUL WEB SITES

http://homepages.unl.ac.uk/~westwelg/filmstudies/sls/slsfaq.htm Film studies at London Metropolitan University is taught using student-led seminars that are clearly described in this web site (accessed 9 June 2003).

http://www.umkc.edu/centers/cad/si/sidocs/siartdex.html The Supplemental Instruction (SI) site offers links to resource material and explanatory papers and articles (accessed 9 June 2003).

VIDEO

Student-led Tutorials, Teaching Support and Media Services, University of Southampton, Teaching Support and Media Services, South Academic Block, Southampton General Hospital, Tremona Road, Southampton SO9 4XY. Telephone (01703) 796563.

Chapter 7

Skill acquisition in SGT

INTRODUCTION

In this chapter we wish to show how SGT can be used to develop a set of nationally recognized key skills that lead towards employability. In particular we also wish to provide a framework for teaching specific psychomotor or practical skills. We will describe the key skills and employability framework and then consider how they can be provided by SGT. This will be followed by a description of the process of acquiring practical skills and the outline of a useful framework for teaching them.

KEY SKILLS

Recommendation 21
We recommend that institutions of higher education begin immediately to develop, for each programme they offer, a 'programme specification' which identifies potential stopping-off points and gives the intended outcomes of the programme in terms of:

■ the knowledge and understanding that a student will be expected to have upon completion;
■ *key skills: communication, numeracy, the use of information technology and learning how to learn;*
■ cognitive skills, such as an understanding of methodologies or ability in critical analysis;
■ *subject specific skills, such as laboratory skills.*

There is much evidence of support for the further development of a range of skills during higher education, including what we term the key skills of communication, both oral and written, numeracy, the use of communications and information technology and learning how to learn. We see these as necessary outcomes of all higher education programmes.

(Dearing 1997: Ch. 9, para. 53; emphasis added)

The nationally agreed set of key skills, recommended above, have been specified in detail by the Qualifications and Curriculum Authority (QCA) and are in the following six areas:

- **communication**
- **application of number**
- **information technology**
- working with others
- improving own learning and performance
- problem solving.

The three key skills in bold have been given particular prominence by the UK government. Further information about these skills is available on the QCA web site (http://www.qca.org.uk).

Each of the six QCA key skills is specified in detail at four levels. Progression through the levels is characterized by:

- increased technical demand
- increased complexity of the context
- increased autonomy of the individual
- increased emphasis on process
- reviewing and critically evaluating.

For example, at level 1 an individual might merely follow clear directions carrying out a simple task whereas at level 4 he or she could be in charge of a complex and lengthy project.

EMPLOYABILITY

It is suggested that the acquisition of key skills leads to 'employability' and to a set of employability skills which most employers feel are mandatory. These are listed here:

 110

- effective communication and interpersonal skills
- analytical, critical and synthetic skills
- teamworking
- problem solving
- using initiative
- self-organization
- time management
- being adaptable and flexible.

In addition another set of skills, which might be termed 'professional' skills, is concerned with reflective practice and the desire to engage in continuing education. Employability can be seen as an attitude towards lifelong learning.

HOW SGT CAN FACILITATE THE ACQUISITION OF KEY SKILLS AND EMPLOYABILITY

As we have shown in previous chapters, the nature of SGT is such that simply engaging in the process develops the whole range of 'key skills' and employability. It is worth listing and referencing them to the chapters where they have been discussed in more detail.

- Communication skills: Chapters 1 and 6
- Teamworking and collaboration: Chapters 1 and 5
- Application and problem solving: Chapters 5 and 11
- Presenting: Chapters 1, 6 and 11
- Researching: Chapters 5, 6 and 11
- Critical evaluation: Chapters 1, 8 and 11
- Metacognition: Chapter 5
- Reflection: Chapters 5, 10 and 11
- Personal development: Chapter 5

TEACHING PRACTICAL SKILLS

Many disciplines in HE require learners to practise and master a variety of manipulative techniques and to use specific pieces of equipment and machinery. Scientific, environmental and engineering subjects all involve the use of a wide range of increasingly sophisticated devices which are essential for modern practice. In the medical and health fields doctors, dentists, nurses and physiotherapists must learn clinical skills which have to be carried out safely and sensitively on patients. These practical skills are often referred to as psychomotor skills (Simpson 1966) since they involve the acquisition of co-ordinated sequences of muscular movements. SGT is an ideal teaching medium for learning practical skills, because it allows the teacher to easily demonstrate the skill, using appropriate methods to be described later, enables important feedback to be given and allows learners to learn from and with each other in a community of novices.

SGT facilitators need to be aware that there are a number of theoretical frameworks that have been put forward to aid in the understanding of psychomotor skills acquisition. In addition there are some recommended procedures that have been developed to optimize the learning of psychomotor skills. Frameworks for understanding the stages by which learners acquire practical skills are described shortly.

THE PSYCHOMOTOR DOMAIN

Simpson (1966) described seven levels that learners can pass through on the way to achieving the highest levels of psychomotor skills.

- Levels one and two include 'perception', where the learner merely identifies the need to perform a particular skill in response to perceptual clues, and 'set' when the learner is ready to act.
- Levels three and four include 'guided response', when the skill is performed immediately after a demonstration, and 'mechanism' when the skill has started to become habitual.
- Level five, or 'complex overt response', is characterized by an accurate and efficient performance of the skill.
- Level six, or 'adaptation', occurs when the skill has been so well internalized that it can be adapted for different contexts and situations.
- Level seven or 'origination' involves the creative development of new psychomotor skills.

Fitts and Posner (1967) break up the sequence of skills learning into three phases:

- the *cognitive* phase when the skill is being learned
- the *associative* phase when performance is becoming skilled
- the *autonomous* phase when the skill has become entirely automatic and can be carried out without thinking about it.

The system described by Miller (outlined below), ranging from 'knows about' to 'does', has been widely used in medical education to describe the stages of clinical learning and to judge levels of competence (Miller 1990).

- *Does:* is a competent and independent practitioner under working conditions
- *Shows how:* demonstrates basic competence under controlled conditions
- *Knows how:* knows how to do a skill and is practising it
- *Knows about:* has knowledge about a skill but is not yet practising it.

A more comprehensive analysis has been provided by Benner (1984) in her book about nursing practice, *From Novice to Expert*. Although more concerned with holistic clinical practice rather than single psychomotor skills, it nevertheless provides a useful framework for seeing how knowledge and attitudes are integrated with psychomotor skills in professional practice. The fundamental process identified for learners is the progression from reliance on abstract principles and rule based behaviour to the increased use of actions based on personal experience. Benner identifies five stages:

- novice
- advanced beginner
- competent
- proficient
- expert.

All these frameworks share a number of concepts in common. In particular there is progression from the purely cognitive through various levels of practice and basic competence to mastery. However, psychomotor skills acquisition is seen to have a strong cognitive and attitudinal component, so it is important to realize that reasons and values frequently underpin the purely physical process of skill acquisition. Although skills are acquired by deliberate and repetitive imitation and practise eventually they become internalized, automatic and capable of modification in different contexts. This latter feature of psychomotor skills can lead to problems when an expert is called upon to teach them to a novice as will be discussed in the next section.

METHODS OF TEACHING SKILLS

Experts may encounter problems when teaching a psychomotor skill because it has become so internalized and their actions have become so smooth, automatic and efficient that they find it difficult to break it down into its component parts. The ability to analyse a skill in this way is absolutely essential and is one of the most important skills a facilitator needs to have if novices are to acquire it. Building on the frameworks described earlier, some tried and tested techniques for teaching psychomotor skills have evolved. First of all, the principles of psychomotor skills learning are described and then a five-step training protocol based on them is outlined (George and Doto 2001).

Conceptualization

Some time should be devoted to the cognitive and attitudinal components that learners should understand prior to the learning of a practical skill. This can provide stimulation and motivation for what might be difficult and challenging activities. The facilitator should put the learning of the skill into context by explaining why participants need to learn it and the reasons for its importance, relevance and usefulness. Learners should be made aware of the skill's degree of difficulty, and roughly how much effort and practice might be required to achieve a specified level of competence. Issues of health and safety and the use of appropriate precautions must be mentioned. In the case of practical skills applied to patients the attitudinal, ethical and communication aspects need to be emphasized.

Visualization

Learners should be able to see the whole skill carried out from start to finish by the expert in normal time. The demonstrator need not provide any verbal explanations of actions at this stage so that the performance is not slowed down in any way. This enables the learner to start to construct an internal mental representation of the expected perform-ance. All equipment should be available and participants should have a clear view of what is going on.

Verbalization

The skill should be demonstrated and explained at the same time. Here the skills of the facilitator in breaking down the skill into its compon-ents become essential. The facilitator should try as much as possible to put him or herself into the position of the novice and try to be aware of the cognitive and manipulative problems they might face. Not only should the facilitator explain the procedure but also the novices should be encouraged to articulate and describe the processes occurring. Their verbal contributions will add to the internal mental representation.

Practice

The novice should be able to practise the skill. It is up to the judge-ment of the facilitator whether a skill needs to be practised as a whole or, in the case of a more complex skill, broken down in to some of its component parts. The amount of practice required will vary with the complexity of the skill. Eventually, however, all the parts will need to be integrated and this process needs to be managed effectively.

Feedback

This very important component of psychomotor skills teaching relies on the skills of the facilitator to give help and guidance to novices. Again it is here that the ability to empathize with learners and to get into their 'mind-set' is essential. Feedback should reward positive actions.

Skill mastery

This phase occurs after much practice and allows the learner to demon-strate to the facilitator that they have achieved a specific level of required competence.

Skill autonomy

This phase constitutes independent practice and means that the learner can routinely perform the skill without error in real-life contexts.

The five-step psychomotor skills teaching protocol

Using the above framework it is possible to develop a basic system that can be applied to the teaching of virtually any psychomotor skill (George and Doto 2001). This is outlined below.

Step 1

Introduce and contextualize the skill to be taught. Activate any prior knowledge or skills by questioning. Explain reasons why the skill is required and its relevance and usefulness. Indicate how long it will take to learn the skill and how much practice might be required. Outline what is going to take place.

Step 2

Demonstrate the skill in real time exactly as it is performed with no verbal commentary.

Step 3

Repeat the demonstration but this time break it down into appropriate sections, explaining what is happening at each stage. Encourage students to ask questions and ensure that they understand what is going on.

Step 4

Students are next asked to guide the facilitator through the skill instructing him or her in what to do at each stage. The facilitator may question the students again and ensure that they understand the process and are giving clear and accurate instructions.

Step 5

The students next practise the skill themselves with the facilitator providing feedback on their progress.

 116

Although this procedure may seem overly formalized, by following it learners will have a much better grasp of what is expected of them when they come to practise the skill. This will potentially reduce the amount of feedback required.

FURTHER READING

Burke, J. (ed.) (1989) *Competency-based Education and Training*, London and New York: Falmer.

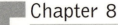

Chapter 8

Using C&IT in SGT

INTRODUCTION

Increasingly computing and information technology (C&IT) is being used in higher education to support teaching and facilitate learning in a wide variety of ways. Many UK students entering higher education have acquired basic IT skills through their work on the National Curriculum at school or in their previous employment and they are expected to develop their skills further during their studies. But to what extent can C&IT be used to specifically support SGT? We will re-examine the aims of SGT (as described earlier) and show that in almost every case C&IT can be used to support the achievement of these aims. In addition we need to recognize that C&IT now enables us to extend the boundaries of conventional SGT both spatially and temporally to include distance learning and asynchronous discussion forums. The use of C&IT may also give the tutor help in managing SGT, organizing classes and giving feedback to students.

AIMS OF SGT

In Chapter 1 the aims of SGT were summarized as:

- the development of intellectual understanding
- the development of intellectual and professional abilities
- the development of communication skills
- personal growth
- professional growth
- support for independence
- the development of group working skills
- reflective practice.

We have seen previously that conventional SGT, with a group of students plus a facilitator, can support all of these aims but it may not be immediately obvious how introducing computers into the relationship can help. If one of the most important conditions for effective SGT is to encourage students to talk to each other, then won't including computers simply create barriers to communication and push students in the direction of independent learning? Isn't a personal computer (PC) by its very nature a tool for the individual? And isn't SGT about group work and interactivity? Clearly the way a PC is used is of crucial importance in maintaining this ethos and achieving the aims of SGT.

What follows is an attempt to briefly summarize some of the ways that C&IT has been used to support SGT. A helpful source of much further information is the ASTER Project (http://cti-psy.york.ac.uk/aster/) based in the Psychology Department at the University of York, where further references to C&IT developments in specific disciplines can be found.

HOW CAN C&IT SUPPORT SGT?

There are many reasons why C&IT has been introduced into courses to support SGT and some of them are summarized here. (It can be seen that there is considerable overlap with the 'Aims of SGT' list at the start of the chapter.)

- to facilitate deep learning
- to practise problem solving
- to develop critical thinking skills
- to encourage and increase participation
- to include tasks that facilitate discussion and writing
- to develop transferable skills
- to encourage teamworking and collaboration.

Tansley and Bryson (2000) have listed the added benefits of virtual learning that have been identified by researchers and those running online discussions and seminars. These are summarized here:

- to provide an opportunity for students to begin at their own starting point and work at their own pace
- to promote learning rather than teaching with the associated shift for the tutor to facilitate rather than provide knowledge

119

- to support collaborative and deep learning
- to encourage increased interaction between students
- to facilitate wider participation and lessen senses of social inequality and the impact of differences in language and spoken communication skills
- to provide a permanent record of learning and interactions that allows students to revisit, reflect upon and revise.

However, the same authors do report that some students are dissatisfied with online tutorials and reported missing the social and educational benefits of face-to-face interaction with their peers and tutors. This clearly needs to be kept in mind when considering the total replacement of 'real' seminars with 'virtual' ones.

The ways in which C&IT can be used in SGT have been grouped into six categories here to assist our discussions, although there is clearly some overlap:

- resources
- interactive learning
- interactive assessment
- electronic communication
- electronic portfolios
- virtual learning environments.

Resources

The fundamental use of electronic resources in SGT is to encourage deeper level understanding, interactivity, collaborative learning and discussion. Students can use C&IT to readily access a plethora of learning resources and information in the form of notes, worksheets, case studies, PBL scenarios, texts, e-books, data sets, web links, information and software. Such resources can be used by students to help them prepare for their classes and, therefore, make class interactions with the tutor and peers more useful. Some classrooms are now set up to enable resources to be accessed and utilized during the session itself to stimulate discussion or provide further data on problems or cases. In the case of PBL tutorials C&IT can be used not only to provide the scenario which initiates the session but also to provide additional information on the problem being considered. In addition the multimedia nature of modern C&IT means that video, audio sequences and animated diagrams can readily be incorporated into learning materials. This broadens the scope of possible resource types and allows examples of practice and real case studies to be available to the students in class.

Accessing such resources through the computer means that the students can hear and see things at their own pace and do so repeatedly if they wish. This can only increase the experiential learning capacity of the group, exposing students to stimulating, exciting and challenging images which are relevant and useful for their appropriate disciplines.

Using the web as a resource

It may also become a particular feature of the SGT session that the reliability and validity of information discovered on the internet can be discussed in class. It is important that students can develop the skills they need to be able to evaluate information gathered in this way. Plagiarism too may be an appropriate and helpful topic for discussion in this context as the world wide web has made plagiarism a more prominent issue in HE.

Interactive learning

It is possible to structure and organize SGT around the use of specific pieces of software, either to teach how to use the software or to use the software as a tool to achieve other learning goals. 'Office' based programs, statistical and data processing packages and conventional computer-assisted learning (CAL) packages can be used in a variety of ways. Students can work individually and then as a group to discuss their experiences, problems and achievements. Alternatively students can work in twos and threes at a computer, talking and interacting with each other while using the program. They can then come together as a larger group at the end of the session to raise wider issues and summarize findings.

Simulations are particularly useful in some disciplines, enabling students to grasp dynamic and complex relationships. Students can more easily understand physical processes, mathematical and statistical concepts and can be exposed to a wider range of problem-solving situations through C&IT based simulations.

For example, in the Business School, a computer-based simulation called 'Chancellor' is used to help groups of students understand the complex way in which variables in macro economics interrelate, e.g.

121

how raising interest rates can impact upon employment rates and investment. The students set goals for their 'virtual economy' and manipulate the possible variables, over a period of several weeks, plotting and discussing the changes they observe in order to work out the connections and relationships. Collaborative learning is encouraged around the computer simulation and students plan and make decisions collectively. It is vital that within the SGT framework the students are encouraged to talk with each other about what they have learned from the simulation and how it relates to theory.

Interactive assessment

C&IT can also be used to co-ordinate formative computer-aided assessment (CAA) either online or via dedicated learning packages. Students can complete self-assessment questionnaires or test questions to test their own level of comprehension or ability and prepare for summative assessments.

For example, when learning about 'concrete', architecture students are asked to complete a computer-based multiple choice, phase test, halfway through the term. The students can use the test once and log a score or they can choose to redo the test, after obtaining online feedback and review their initial answers. Tutors on the course can monitor the progress of their tutees and using the management information from the whole class test results, can provide direct feedback on progress and suggest remedial actions during SGT sessions.

Students clearly value the opportunities to 'self-test' that computer-based quizzes and online tests provide.

 The quiz tests help you practise doing tests which makes you more confident in the real thing.

Better than reading a book, more interactive, makes you think.

The quiz tests tell you where you are going wrong and show weaknesses.

(Students' comments on the benefits of computer-based quiz tests quoted in Exley 2001: 6)

But this is taking us beyond the focus of this book and Paul Chin's book on *Using C&IT to Support Teaching* (2004) in this series can provide further detail here.

 122

Electronic communication

Although SGT places a strong emphasis on direct interpersonal communication, C&IT systems now make it possible to develop alternative modes of communication that can extend the spatial and temporal boundaries of group learning. Students and facilitators can now communicate directly via email and groups of students, on defined courses, can interact in chat rooms (synchronously) or via bulletin boards (asynchronously).

This can take place as the result of a specific SGT session or it can be initiated online to encourage a virtual discussion as a preliminary to a real SGT session. There are even specialized programs, such as the Merlin system (developed at the University of Hull) that can provide resources to students and then manage an asynchronous virtual, discussion group (see example at the end of this chapter). This thinking can be extended through the use of tele-conferencing or digital video-conferencing, to enable synchronous discussion between learners who are geographically separated (see Figure 8.1).

Different educational strategies, such as work-based learning or problem based learning, can provide the learning frameworks in which

FIGURE 8.1 Talking heads

technology can support students who are working 'at a distance'. Although face-to-face communication between students or between students and facilitators may be minimized in these situations the benefits of interpersonal communication, analysis and reflection are preserved. Distance learning can be individualized to meet the professional and personal needs of students and provide flexibly timetabled learning for a wide variety of learners. As greater numbers of mature learners and part-time students enter HE, such flexibility in course design and methods of facilitating discussion and tutor support will be increasingly necessary.

The growth in undergraduate student numbers has increased the size of many classes and placed further pressure on small group teaching. Many of the new ways of integrating and using C&IT can, potentially, compensate for the lack of social cohesion and interactivity that can be the by-product of such expansion. However, this can be achieved only with thoughtful planning and the development of C&IT approaches that allow students to work together and value that interaction (through the assessment scheme if necessary).

Electronic portfolios

Portfolios are increasingly being used by students in HE to record learning experiences and to provide evidence of review and critical reflection. Electronic portfolios are merely an electronic extension of this concept. When integrated in SGT they can be used to encourage students to discuss their experiences and personal development. Making certain sections of the electronic portfolio 'public' enables other students and the facilitator to monitor and respond to reflections by means of a discussion forum. Once again the use of C&IT can extend the boundaries of interpersonal communication.

Electronic portfolios can be used to support personal tutoring and the facilitation of student personal development plans (PDPs) or progress development files (PDFs). The sector-wide use of student PDFs was recommended in the Dearing report (1997); the Quality Assurance Agency together with the universities issued a policy statement which said that PDPs should be introduced and operating for all students by 2005.

Progress Files should consist of two elements: a transcript recording student achievement which should follow a common format devised by institutions collectively through their representative bodies; a means by which students can monitor, build and reflect upon their personal development.

(http://www.qaa.ac.uk/crntwork/progfileHE/contents.htm)

For example, the Learning and Teaching Support Network (LTSN) Centre for Engineering at the University of Loughborough is supporting the development and dissemination of an electronically based PDF called 'Rapid' Progress Files. Students are required to record their achievements and the skills they have developed together with other more factually based information, such as the course modules they have attended etc. The PDF has a strong focus on the final production of *curricula vitae* for individual students, however, the process of recording and reflecting on personal development and continuing professional development can be best supported through a form of personal tutoring and SGT. Many departments are seeking to integrate the personal use of PDFs within a framework of group tutorials, to provide ongoing guidance and support for the students in using the files effectively and to monitor and assess their impact.

Virtual learning environments

All of the systems described above can be incorporated into an electronic virtual learning environment. In a VLE the provision of teaching information and resources, discussion forums, CAA and electronic portfolios can be integrated into one package for a whole course, including timetables, contact information and so on. Students and teachers can gain electronic access to the resources for a whole curriculum. From a student's perspective this encourages both horizontal and vertical learning integration and enables students to take more responsibility for their learning as they can see the 'big picture'. From the tutor's perspective it makes it much easier to make all curriculum resources available to the group so enriching the learning environment.

Running virtual tutorials

Elwyn *et al.* (2001) have identified some potential problems in running virtual groups that facilitators should be aware of.

125

Dependence on technology

Clearly for virtual groups to function effectively, the members must be reasonably familiar with basic C&IT skills, such as how to use a PC, send email and use the internet. Most students entering HE these days have these skills but facilitators should be aware of any students who need extra help and ensure that they receive appropriate guidance. In the same way that students in conventional SGT need to develop their oral communication skills students in virtual groups need to know how to use the technology if they are to interact and communicate effectively.

Absence of non-verbal clues in communication

It has been said that 80 per cent of all conventional interpersonal communication is non-verbal. In virtual groups, where students communicate asynchronously in writing via email, or in discussion forums and chat rooms, this non-verbal communication is lost. However, Salmon (1997) has identified a set of alternative skills that can be developed to partially compensate for the loss of face-to face contact; these are listed in Table 8.1. It is important to realize that these virtual communication skills can be taught and developed.

TABLE 8.1 Stages that a student will go through when developing online group working skills

- **Level 1 Gaining access**
  Is able to log on and is motivated to continue. Posts first 'joining' message when instructed.
- **Level 2 Becoming familiar with the online environment**
  Possesses basic technical skills and is confident in sending and receiving messages to and from the group.
- **Level 3 Seeking and giving information**
  Is confident in using all the features of the software. Freely offers, receives and processes information from others online.
- **Level 4 Knowledge construction**
  Demonstrates actions likely to lead to 'knowledge construction' online, including creative and active thinking (asking challenging questions, reflecting, suggesting ideas) and interactive thinking (critiquing, negotiating, interpreting, proposing actions).
- **Level 5 Autonomy and development**
  Takes responsibility for own continuing development in online learning. Is able to set up and support own virtual group.

Using emoticons

'Emoticons' (http://www.computeruser.com/resources/dictionary/
emoticons.html) and other text-based metaphors for non-verbal communication can also be incorporated into emails and postings to give added
empathy, warmth or emotional context. If you haven't seen these before,
tilt your head over to the left and the 'faces' depicted by the text emerge.

:)	A happy person
: (	A sad person
:-D	A laughing person
;-)	A person winking
: -O	Surprised

The term 'netiquette' is sometimes used to describe the skills and
abilities needed to communicate effectively and 'politely' online (Zimmer
and Alexander 1996), the essence of which can be summarized by the
question about 'talking' online:

'Would you say it to a person's face or write it on a postcard?'

Language or cultural barriers

Members of virtual groups may share different cultures or even speak
different languages, creating further communication problems. However, if certain ground rules are agreed to, then major problems can be
avoided. For example it might be agreed that the language of communication will be English, that slang or vernacular expressions will be
avoided, that abbreviations and acronyms will always be spelled out
when first used and that references to specific cultural or social factors
will be briefly explained.

Asynchronous versus synchronous interaction

Whereas conventional SGT involves synchronous communication, with
the exception of online chat, virtual group work is mainly asynchronous with group members logging on at a time convenient to them.
Although this minimises spontaneity it has the benefit of encouraging a
greater degree of reflection and even allows people who might be reticent
in small groups to make a thoughtful contribution to the discussion.

127

Two of the quietest students in class turned out to be real stars online. I think the positive reactions from the other students has made them feel more confident. I have noticed that one of them, in particular, seems happier to talk in the class now and I can always pick up on things that they have said online as a way of drawing them into class discussions too.

(From an e-tutor in the International Relations Department)

When many teaching staff first engage with online communication and discussion boards they often assume that just creating the environment is enough and wonder why students then don't engage. The most important point I would say, particularly with group work, is to provide an incentive for the students, whether it is through assessment and gaining marks or to generate something that the students need or value. I found (or rather, the students did) being online once a week at a specified time was extremely helpful and because we had shared whiteboard technology it had that novel feel to it which the students found 'interesting'. [Shared whiteboards are like flip charts or notepads, and what you draw on your PC linked pad also appears on other PCs and other people can add to your notes/drawings.]

(From an e-tutor in the Chemistry Department)

MANAGING ONLINE DISCUSSIONS

Online, should you leave your students to get on with it or do you need to intervene sometimes in order to manage and referee the exchange? The roles a tutor may need to carry out are outlined here (adapted from Shepherd 2003).

Set the rules at the start

Check that the students are happy with

- the mechanics of using the software
- the topics that are appropriate for online discussion
- how new topics are initiated
- understand issues of netiquette and rules for acceptable behaviour online.

Initiate discussion topics

As with live discussions, it takes someone to get things started. Many students will prefer to read other people's messages rather than to write and post up communications themselves and, if that's the case, the facility will be unused.

You can stimulate the use of online exchanges by initiating topics that all your students will be interested in or need to understand for course assessments:

Appeal to their life experiences, vested interests and ambitions.

(Dr W. R. Klemm 1998)

Encourage students to initiate their own discussions

A discussion facility is useful as a way of resolving the particular queries and problems of individual students. Encourage students to make use of peer support in this way – make it clear that this isn't considered to be 'cheating'.

Refocus discussions that are going off course

While not wanting to discourage social interaction between students, sometimes discussions can go so far off the point that the intended learning outcomes for the discussion will not be achieved. If you see this happening, you need to send a message that gently refocuses the discussion.

Summarize learning points

It is beneficial for the tutor to summarize the key points that have been raised and any conclusions reached at several stages in the discussion. You can then redirect the discussion or, if it has run its useful course, bring it to an end.

Act quickly to prevent inappropriate communications

Occasionally the rules that you establish for the discussion will be broken and students will expect you to take action to remedy the situation. It may be that discussions have become over-heated or insensitive, or offensive language is being used. It all depends on what your rules are, of course, but if they are broken, you should act quickly to solve the problem.

As in face-to-face situations, it is not appropriate to discipline people in public. Use private email, the telephone or better still a face-to-face meeting to address the issue directly with any students involved.

Prune out dead topics

You only need to keep useful messages as an archive for future students. The rest can be deleted once the flow of discussion has moved on.

Require participation

Dr W. R. Klemm, writing in the guidance given in support of the VLE, Blackboard Inc. (http://www.blackboard.com) suggests:

> Don't let it be optional. Set aside a portion of the grade allocation for participation in the online discussions. Tell the students that they must post x number of items each week or for each topic. Critics will say that this approach does nothing to ensure quality of input. But it at least gets the students engaged, and hopefully, once they get caught up in the activity, they will strive to improve the relevance and quality of their work, because now they are on display. No longer can they hide. For many students, it is more embarrassing to make public postings that have no value. As another incentive for quality work, the teacher can grade on quality of the postings using clear and transparent criteria.

Working as an online tutor

Ryan et al. (2000) suggest that the online tutor is an educational facilitator who 'contributes specialist knowledge and insight, focuses the discussion on the critical points, asks questions and responds to students' contributions, weaves together disparate comments and synthesises the points made to foster emerging themes'. All of which look very familiar and mirror the role of a face-to-face tutor. Barker (2002) suggests that the role can often be broader and include aspects of pastoral tutoring and assessment too.

In the future, it is likely that many teachers in HE and FE will be required to act as virtual tutors. It is appreciated that there will be a need for updating tutor skills to operate effectively online and that appropriate VLEs be designed which can support the aims of SGT in practice.

EXAMPLES FROM DIFFERENT DISCIPLINES

Group work in an IT module

Students take a module to develop their basic IT skills in MS Office (word processing etc.). As part of the PowerPoint (PP) work we try to help them develop their transferable skills, their presentation skills and group working skills in particular. They are given some content and relevant web links with which to produce a PP presentation. Students work in groups of between three and five to produce a group presentation. Their work is assessed on the basis of three things, on the content, their IT skills and evidence of group working. They have to use the VLE (in this case Blackboard) to communicate online and to share work. Since the groups are often made up of students who cannot meet regularly because of timetable clashes, they must share and develop work online and this can then also act as evidence in support of their group working assessment.

Group work is measured for each person in terms of their individual contribution to the presentation but the whole group can also be penalized if they cannot provide evidence that they have tried to support and encourage each other. The technology acts as a facilitator for sharing work, ideas and (dare we say it) evidence that group work has actually taken place. The practical advantages include being able to work under constraints (can't meet in person), being able to work at all times of day and night because of access to the technology and the other usual advantages associated with face-to-face group work.

Group work and experimental simulations in ecology

We use the VLE, Blackboard and a piece of software called Simlife, which simulates ecological scenarios such as predator–prey interrelationships and the affects of global warming. The students are put into groups of three to five and are given an ecological scenario to work on, which they have to investigate using the software. All the necessary materials, notes and resources are provided online through Blackboard. Several groups do the same scenario so that they can make comparisons with other groups. The students collaborate online, sharing ideas and using discussion forums to discuss their work and results. The simulation is run over three weeks and they can work on it at any time. I use Blackboard to log on for a specified hour each week so that the students can communicate with me synchronously. In real terms this has saved me two hours of contact teaching a week.

The students produce a group report at the end but they also write an action plan at the start of the simulation. The action plan is anonymously marked and commented on by the other student groups to help groups refine their planning. The group report also has a component of peer assessment in it. Each group member assesses the contribution of the other members and submits marks anonymously. Marks and comments are all delivered electronically.

Using a VLE to support SGT on a learning and teaching course: 'Merlin'

Some VLEs (e.g. WebCT and Blackboard) emphasize a content delivery approach. We are using a VLE called Merlin that is based on the importance of student interaction in learning. This suits the student-centred philosophy of our course in learning and teaching and seems particularly relevant to advanced level courses (in this case a postgraduate certificate).

Merlin's strength is that it allows the course team to do more than merely post materials to the web. Tutors can use learning pathways to build learning *stages* for the students to work through and use an e-portfolio as a personal space for student's work items. Each year we have approximately fifty students, but we can use the virtual space to enable several much smaller groups to work together; we call these learning sets. Students in learning sets can supplement and replace face-to-face meetings by working together virtually in the discussion areas provided by Merlin.

Flexibility on the learning pathway

Each stage in the pathway is a guided study route, with a series of tasks to complete that involve reading, summarizing, discussing, evaluating, analysing, synthesizing and so on. Some of these tasks are done outside Merlin (e.g. reading might include links to web sites) while others are hosted within Merlin (e.g. discussions and peer critique of work). We can be flexible in how the groups choose to work, for example by running a particular stage two or three times a year, or by running it whenever participants gather themselves into a viably sized group of six people. Key benefits are that students can learn at their own pace (within limits) and they can work with staff who are not necessarily at our university but who will 'meet' with them virtually in the discussion areas at specified times.

Peer critique using the portfolio

In one particular stage we ask students to write a short piece to summarize their views on learning and teaching. They save this work item in their personal portfolio and share it with the course tutors to indicate that they have completed the task. After the deadline, the tutors ask each participant to use Merlin to share their work item with three named participants, and to comment on the portfolio items that others share with them. In this way each participant will not only receive a critique of their own work, but also see the work of others and have an opportunity to interact with their opinions and ideas.

Online problem based learning in medicine

This is a VLE for supporting medical PBL groups working synchronously in a university environment. Conventional PBL groups of seven or eight students use a database of educational resources in their base room to facilitate their learning through a two-year PBL curriculum constructed around forty or so scenarios. The VLE supplies them with their weekly scenario to initiate their PBL session. Then for each scenario it provides them with online access to appropriate and relevant basic medical science information, clinical data, images of patients or X-rays. These data are designed to help students solve the problems they have given themselves and achieve the learning outcomes for each scenario. Providing online access to information in this way speeds up the PBL process but does not preclude students from using more conventional sources of data such as libraries and even members of staff.

133

Supporting online collaborative learning at a distance

Attempting to achieve SGT learning goals in online distance learning is still an active area of development and no one system has yet been globally adopted. One system, the Asynchronous Collaboration Tool (ACT: Duffy *et al.* 1999), has been developed specifically to work with PBL groups in distance learning. It consists of a discussion space that is organized using either threads or a linear arrangement of messages. It allows users to post emails to each other tagged with previously defined labels to reinforce metacognitive involvement in the discussion. SenseMaker (Hoadley and Bell 1996) works by allowing students to group sets of links to information using a visual structure that allows clear visual delineation of positions or ideas. Knowledge Forums, developed by the Computer Supported Intentional Learning Environments group (CSILE) in Toronto uses agents that can be attached to messages in a rich, visual, knowledge-building environment that fosters a natural communication of ideas through interconnected networks that learners can visually rearrange.

A more recent development is Groove Workspace (http://www.groove.net/) which is a 'desktop collaboration software' that uses email and Microsoft Office for online synchronous small group interaction. It enables users to share files and work with others on documents, tasks, projects and decisions in a virtual shared space. Although originally designed for business use, it is ideally suited to facilitate online PBL and collaborative learning. When participants have arranged to be online together, via email, they enter the virtual shared space where they can engage in synchronous online chat or direct sound messaging. In this space they can simultaneously look at documents produced by Microsoft Office applications or images and can manipulate or annotate resources using a variety of tools such as pens and pointers.

📖 FURTHER READING

Chin, P. (2003) *Using C&IT to Support Teaching*, London: RoutledgeFalmer.

Elwyn, G., Greenhalgh, T. and Macfarlane, F. (2001) *Groups: A Guide to Small Group Work in Healthcare, Management, Education and Research*, Oxford: Radcliffe Medical Press.

Ryan, S., Freeman, H., Scott, B. and Patel, D. (2000) *The Virtual University: The Internet and Resource-Based Learning*, London: Kogan Page.

Tansley, C. and Bryson, C. (2000) 'Virtual seminars – a viable substitute for traditional approaches?', *Innovations in Education and Training International* 27(4): 323–35.

USEFUL WEB SITES

http://cti-psy.york.ac.uk/aster ASTER Project. This site provides information and resources to support the use of C&IT in small group teaching and learning. It has a growing bibliography of research articles and books that can be searched or browsed by discipline or teaching activity (accessed 9 June 2003).

http://www.albion.com/netiquette/ This site is dedicated to 'netiquette' and promoting effective and polite online communication (accessed 9 June 2003).

http://rapid.lboro.ac.uk/ 'Rapid Progress Files' (accessed 9 June 2003).

http://www.fastrak-consulting.co.uk/tactix/ Tactix: tips and tools for trainers and communicators. This site includes a range of useful online articles including Shepherd, C. (2000) 'The asynchronous online tutor' (accessed 9 June 2003).

Chapter 9

Syndicate classes and workshops

INTRODUCTION

The purpose of this chapter is to discuss the overall organization, sequencing and design of small group teaching sessions in the context of larger teaching events such as syndicate classes, workshops and away days. It will look at how a variety of small group teaching techniques may fit within a larger framework and show, by means of specific examples, how session plans may vary from one discipline to another.

SYNDICATE CLASSES

Conventionally SGT groups have a facilitator but an alternative technique involves using syndicate groups which are tutor-less independent learning groups. Although considerable facilitation and organization are required to set them up, once they are implemented they can operate without significant intervention to achieve specified learning goals. A body of students is split up into groups of five or six who work in a self-directed and co-ordinated manner on specific tasks which might involve reading, discussion and/or the production of written assignments. These activities occur during regular timetabled sessions, which may replace lectures. Syndicate groups may work on different tasks and then present their findings during plenary sessions during the course. The facilitator's role is to co-ordinate this process, ensure that groups are 'on task' and that appropriate outcomes are reached for all students at the end of the course. Examples of some syndicate classes, their organization and content are given in this chapter.

WORKSHOPS

Workshops are extended SGT sessions, often lasting a morning, an afternoon or a whole day, orientated towards the achievement of a specific set of outcomes involving active participation. They consist of a series of linked SGT activities which need to be embedded in an overall curriculum framework and co-ordinated to ensure that participants feel comfortable with the overall process, that they have their learning needs more or less fulfilled and they all engage in a variety of useful, relevant and stimulating activities.

The structure and activities within a workshop should be carefully planned, co-ordinated and timed. Practical arrangements, such as having an appropriate number of rooms of appropriate size, ensuring there are enough breaks and that refreshments are provided are equally important and reference to Maslow's hierarchy of needs is a useful framework to use when planning (see Table 2.1, p. 16). Many of the techniques previously described can be used and a generic workshop framework is provided here.

Preparation

Participants should be clear on the nature and proposed outcomes of the workshop in any pre-workshop documentation. If necessary they should be given instructions on any preparation that might be required. This could include reading relevant documents, thinking about a list of specific issues or preparing a mini-presentation or demonstration.

Arriving

Participants should be given accurate information on where to come and at what time. The location of the registration area should be well signposted from a variety of directions. On arrival participants could be given information packs containing course materials, references, timetables, room maps, room numbers and name badges. At this stage there should be an opportunity to meet informally.

Overview

The workshop may begin with a plenary session at which the aims and outcomes are stated, maybe a brief address from a key-note speaker followed by a description of the workshop activities, including plenary sessions, breaks and other housekeeping information.

Grouping

A variety of techniques (see Chapter 4) are available for breaking large groups up into smaller groups and these may be used at this stage.

Introductions and ice-breaking

Once groups have been formed, if the grouping process did not include an element of personal introductions, this should be initiated at this stage and coupled to an ice-breaking activity. These need to be co-ordinated by SGT facilitators who are either supplied to or recruited from within the group.

SGT activities

A variety of SGT activities should be used relevant to the proposed outcomes that have been set. These have previously been discussed in Chapter 4, with further activities described below. The aim should be the active participation of all group members in keeping with their own learning styles (Honey 1982) and teamworking styles (Belbin 1993). Clear instructions, timings and outcomes should be given and facilitators should time manage effectively so that the work of all the groups remains co-ordinated.

Breaks

Breaks are actually one of the most important features of a workshop. They are where participants can unwind, talk informally to each other and network. Therefore it is essential that an adequate amount of time is set aside for them and that an appropriate level of refreshment is provided. Ensure that individual food and drink preferences are catered for.

Plenaries

Plenaries may introduce a workshop and may act as a point of closure. Most workshops will have plenary sessions were presentations are made by specific individuals or the results of SGT are brought back to the larger group for presentation or discussion. As didactic episodes in an otherwise active learning environment, their timing should be carefully controlled.

Evaluation

Like all forms of teaching workshops should be evaluated and some form of evaluation questionnaire should be filled in at the end. Questionnaires can be given out with the course materials or handed out or placed on seats prior to the plenary. Participants are often reluctant to fill these in so to ensure a good response it is useful to make the questionnaire as brief as possible and to include time at the end of the proceedings for completion.

EXAMPLES OF SYNDICATE CLASS AND WORKSHOP DESIGN

Six outlines of syndicate class and workshop design are described and commented on in this section.

- A case-study workshop in business studies
- A problems class in a mathematical subject
- A syndicate class in education
- Forming, storming, norming and reforming with general practitioners
- A SWOT analysis on Faculty Office development.

Do take a look at all the scenarios as different points about session planning will be raised in each.

A case-study workshop in business studies

The context

The course on 'Strategic planning' has a lecture and a seminar each week. At the end of a lecture the students are provided with two short case studies that describe how two different companies operate. In rotation, two pairs of students are responsible for beginning the seminar each week.

The aim of the seminar is to apply theoretical frameworks to real business examples through the interpretation and analysis or case studies. It is also intended that the students should further develop their oral presentation and group working skills.

Seminars are attended by about sixteen students. The seminar room is quite small, with a large central table that makes it difficult to move the furniture.

Time Seminar plan

2.00   The tutor welcomes the class and briefly introduces the topic by drawing reference to the course outline and handbook. The tutor double checks that all the students have today's case studies with them. (They were made available, in hard copy, in the previous lecture but the department is keen to move towards supplying handouts over the intranet for the students to download for themselves.)

2.05   One pair of students, who have previously been asked to prepare, are invited to briefly summarize the first case study (about Company A) and to identify and report three key features that relate to this week's topic (e.g. 'What internal processes do companies use to make strategic decisions?').

2.10   The second pair of students repeat this process and present key features from the second case study about Company B. The tutor thanks the students and, if necessary, tactfully corrects any significant errors or misleading comments.

2.15   The tutor then sets the questions for the class, based upon the case studies and presentations. This format varies from week to week but today the tutor organizes a 'debate'.

The debate

Introducing the task. Half of the students, sitting on the left side of the table, are asked to support Company A and the other half of the class, on the right, are asked to support Company B.

2.20   To prepare for the debate the students must identify and list the strengths of their company (A) and the weaknesses of the other company (B) or vice versa. To do this the tutor asks the students to discuss the case studies, in small groups of about three, and asks one member of each group to keep a note of important points.

2.35 The debate is chaired by the tutor, who asks Company A supporters to state the strengths of their company's approach. The tutor may also raise additional points at this stage. Then Company B supporters comment on the weaknesses they see in Company A's processes and discussion can take place if students disagree.

2.45 The process is repeated for Company B.

2.55 The tutor summarizes some of the important features of a strategic planning process, drawing upon examples identified by the students, and indicates where the students can read more about the topic in the course textbook.

3.00 Seminar finishes.

Comments

Having two students responsible for presenting the case study introduction provides a safety net for the tutor if one student doesn't turn up to class. The debate section of the seminar could be simplified to be a discussion of strengths and weaknesses in both companies or generate a poster of how best to make strategic decisions using examples from the two companies.

A problems class in a mathematical subject

The context

Thirty students are attending a one-hour problems class as part of their physics undergraduate course. The class runs at 11.00 on a Wednesday morning. The room is laid out with a number of small tables around which four or five students can sit and work together.

The students were given the problem sheet, containing five questions, in the previous class and asked to answer the first two as homework and bring their solutions to class.

The problem set

The first two problems are very straightforward and basically test whether the student has understood the method described in the previous class. Having to do these questions at home before the class encourages the students to reread their notes and the textbook and makes sure that the students come to class prepared to tackle more difficult problems in a supportive environment. The next three questions are to be worked on collaboratively in class by the tables of students. They are three linked questions that progressively increase in complexity and difficulty.

The tutor intends that the students will work together in class, and help each other to solve the more difficult questions. The tutor expects that all the class should be able to answer questions 1 to 4 but that only some of the groups will manage to solve question 5. This question will be challenging to the most able students in the class and the tutor poses the questions in a way that makes this clear to the students. The tutor wishes to stretch the most able students in the class as well as support the students who struggle.

Time   Session plan

11.00   The tutor briefly reintroduces the problem set and re-emphasizes that all should aim to satisfactorily complete the work up to and including question 4. If time remains, groups should tackle question 5.

11.05   The tutor asks the class if they had any difficulty with questions 1 and 2. The tutor displays the solutions to both questions on two overhead projectors and asks the students from one table to swap and mark the homework answers from the students at an adjacent table.

11.15   The students get their marked questions back and can see if they have made any errors or if they haven't properly understood (in which case the tutor will spend some time individually with students in class).

11.20   The tutor then asks the whole class to begin working on question 3 together and reminds the students that they should make sure each person at the table is understanding each step of the problem.

11.35   The tutor asks the class to help work out an answer at the blackboard by inviting suggestions and asking tables to put forward parts of the solution in turn. The tutor then moves around the class double checking that all are happy to move on to question 4.

11.40   The tutor asks the students to work at their own pace for the next fifteen minutes and to get as far through questions 4 and 5 as they can together. Some groups work much faster than others.

11.55   The tutor joins each group briefly and gives them copies of the solutions for questions 4 and 5 on a handout. The students are asked to compare their approach with the model answer given and there is a brief opportunity for questions.

12.00   Class finishes. Any student who wishes to can follow up the class by visiting the tutor's 'office hour' or 'drop-in surgery' the following day.

Comments

The class is quite diverse in terms of the ability of the students and so the problem set is designed to try to provide support for all the students. However, care does need to be taken to ensure that weaker students do not feel overwhelmed by the difficulty of the questions 4 and 5. Here the tutor needs to be sensitive to different needs and move between the tables prompting and asking questions.

The design of the workshop is to give maximum time for group working and collaborative problem solving and to minimize the time given for the tutor's formal presentation of solutions. This will demand active facilitation skills from the tutor as some students may have the expectation that the tutor's role is to go through solutions for all the questions at the board.

A syndicate class in education

The context

There are forty students in the class and the room is flat with movable chairs. The students have recently completed their first placement activity working in a school. This two-hour syndicate workshop is a review session for the placement learning and the aim is to build the confidence of the students and to enable them to share their experiences of being in the classroom for the first time. There are too many students in the group to try and run a whole class discussion and so the strategy is to run syndicate group exercises that will encourage more students to actively participate.

Time *Session plan*

10.00 Welcome and introduction to the learning outcomes for the session which are given as follows.

At the end of the workshop you should be able to

■ reflect upon your experience of working with a class teacher to prepare, organize and facilitate a Literacy hour discussion
■ relate your observations and practice to the theory of course design previously discussed in the course
■ address the questions or concerns you may have about facilitating a discussion with the children.

10.05 In pairs the tutor asks the students to reflect on one high and one low from their placement week in schools.

10.10 The tutor collects about five examples of highs and lows on to a flip chart to show that the group have common concerns and to flag some of the successes to build confidence.

10.15 The tutor gives a short recap on the educational theory of course design and relates it to planning a particular learning session. The tutor introduces the example of planning a Literacy hour session, as this will be a common experience for all the students.

10.30 The tutor asks the pairs of students to join with a second pair (snowball) and compare their 'teaching practice' experiences to the theory. When the groups of four have had chance to talk together for about five minutes the tutor then asks the groups to prepare to report back to the whole group. The students on one side of the room are asked to think of one example where theory and practice seemed to be in harmony and the students on the other side are asked to identify one example where theory and practice appeared to differ.

10.40 The tutor asks one person from each group to report back and tries to respond and link the points raised. The tutor would try to comment on why theory and practice may differ.

10.50 The tutor then explains how the students will work together to ask and respond to questions that have arisen from the work placement. The focus is on 'How to lead a useful discussion with children during the Literacy hour' session.

The task

The tutor gives each group of four students a few sticky Post-it notes and asks each student to write up at least one of their questions, one per Post-it note (they can do more if they wish).

11.00 The group then stick up their notes on to a large sheet of flip chart paper. One group exchanges their sheet with another group and they try to answer each other's questions – or at least offer possible solutions. The groups arrange and, if necessary, cluster the questions around common themes and then write their 'possible solutions' around each Post-it on the flip chart paper.

11.15 The groups then swap sheets back to the question originators, read the suggestions and continue to add their own responses to their own questions.

11.25 The exercise finishes with each group putting up their flip chart on the wall and inviting the students to move around the 'posters' and view the other questions and answers. The students are encouraged by the tutor to make a note of any of the questions and responses that are relevant to them.

The end

11.30 The tutor shows an OHP transparency of the learning outcomes for the session and checks with the students to see if they feel that they have been achieved.
The tutor thanks the students for their hard work and dismisses the class.

145

Comments

The approaches chosen for this workshop place a great emphasis on sharing experiences and aim to build confidence. The integration of theory and practice is discussed and the tutor's inputs link to other parts of the course, such as the lectures and online discussion. The students are encouraged to play a big role in 'answering their own questions' by using their problem-solving and evaluative skills but this is done with the support and guidance of the tutor.

The tutor has several roles during the class, being an information giver, facilitator and monitor, checking that the students are on task and keeping the class to time. The latter being a challenge with a talkative and responsive group of students.

Forming, storming, norming and reforming with general practitioners

The context

The focus of this workshop was to introduce the concept of PBL to a group of postgraduate GP trainers with the aim of encouraging them to use it as a learning technique for trainee GPs.

Time   Session plan

9.00   The workshop began with a general plenary introduction describing the reasons why the group had met, the aims of the meeting and the overall procedure to be followed.

9.20   A twenty-minute presentation using PowerPoint and a data projector on the nature and rationale for PBL.

9.40   A fifteen-minute videotape presentation of an edited PBL session exemplifying the main features.

9.55   Fifteen minutes of questions

10.10   Coffee break.

10.30   *Forming*: still in the large group the first workshop activity was explained so that participants were in no doubt what they were expected to do and to achieve and were aware of the time scale involved. Participants were split up into four groups of ten, choosing a volunteer co-ordinator, and went off to work in separate rooms with a flip chart. (A variety of techniques can be used to do this depending on the agenda: see Chapter 4.)

Each group engaged in an ice-breaking and introduction activity with the co-ordinator acting as a chairperson and keeping the group on task.

10.45 *Storming:* once group members felt comfortable with their group the co-ordinator focused them on the task of brainstorming and discussing issues surrounding the feasibility of developing, implementing and evaluating PBL in general practice training. A series of questions and problems had been provided by the main facilitator. The group co-ordinator recorded the results of this activity on a flip chart. During this process the main facilitator came round and visited each group in turn to ensure the task was being carried out correctly and to co-ordinate timing.

11.30 *Norming:* the results of the brainstorming and discussion were reformulated into conclusions and/or proposals. Since the results of this activity needed to be shared with the other groups a flip chart or overhead acetate was prepared for display and presentation.

12.00 *Reforming:* groups presented their conclusions followed by questions and a general discussion led by the main facilitator. A consensus on the way forward was agreed.

1.00 **Lunch**

2.00 Presentation on constructing PBL scenarios, with examples.

2.45 Group activities: five groups of eight participants created with new group co-ordinators using an appropriate method (see Chapter 4). Brief introductions followed by focused activity on creating PBL scenarios with possible learning outcomes.

3.45 Tea break.

4.00 Group presentations of PBL scenarios.

4.50 General discussion.

147

5.15   Closure and evaluation. The facilitator reviews the objectives of the workshop and summarizes the main outcomes from the group activities.

A SWOT analysis on Faculty Office development

The context

The Faculty Office consists of sixteen administrative, secretarial and academic staff members. Due to both an increase in student numbers and a greater variety of student types in recent years the work of the Faculty Office is becoming strained and there is concern that it is not delivering the service it should to staff and students. The purpose of this SWOT workshop is to use the expertise within the Faculty Office to reformulate its objectives and to develop new working practices that will be more efficient and helpful to its target customers.

Time   *Session plan*

9.00   Introduction to the morning by facilitator and outline of the problems faced by the Faculty Office.

9.15   Meeting split into two groups of eight in the same room followed by simultaneous ice-breaker activity.

9.30   Facilitator proposes to whole meeting that change is required. Faculty Office staff are then offered the chance to participate in developing new working practices. The SWOT analysis process is next outlined.

9.40   Each group of eight works in turn on its strengths and weaknesses (thirty minutes each). Groups record outcomes on a piece of flip chart paper and the facilitator moves between the two groups helping them to formulate their thoughts and to keep focused on the problems and tasks identified.

10.40   Coffee break.

11.00   Each group of eight works in turn on its opportunities and threats (thirty minutes each). Groups record outcomes on a piece of flip chart paper and the facilitator moves between the two groups helping them to formulate their thought and to keep focused on the problems and tasks identified.

12.00 Group discussion. The facilitator guides the group to identify key issues that need to be dealt with utilizing the strengths of the group to maximize the opportunities presented. A prioritized list of proposed changes is produced plus a development strategy.

13.00 Closure.

AWAY DAYS

An away day is a particular type of SGT workshop which takes place away from the normal working environment. This is done to minimize the distractions of telephones, emails and other interruptions so participants can more readily focus on specific issues and problems. By changing the environmental context, groups of people can work together in different ways, exploring new ideas, encouraging creative thinking and building new team relationships. Away days allow participants to spend time together socially as well as working through a variety of SGT methods in both formal and informal settings.

Away days need to be organized, structured and facilitated in the ways already described for workshops but arrangements can be more flexible and the environment can play a greater role. For example encouraging people to work together in groups, as in 'team-building' exercises, might involve performing a physical outdoor task. Buzz groups, where people discuss issues with each other in twos and threes, no longer need to be fixed in a room but can take place sitting under a tree or walking down a country lane.

Away days are ideally suited for the development of teams and for re-visioning exercises where participants ask themselves the questions 'Where are we now?', 'Where are we heading?', 'How are we going to get there?' and 'What might help or hinder us along the way?'

FURTHER READING

Moon, J. (2001) *Short Courses and Workshops*, London: Kogan Page.

Chapter 10

Student diversity in SGT

INTRODUCTION

In a small group the tutor is responsible for making the mode of study appropriate and applicable to all the students in the class. Our global and accessible universities offer the opportunity for a greater mix of people than ever before. People from different countries and educational cultures join the SGT session with widely varying expectations of how to work in a tutorial or problems class. Some students may join the class expecting the tutor to 'lecture' and may find it very difficult to 'challenge' or 'question' what the tutor says because they have no previous experience of formalized collaborative learning.

The tutor must work to make the class a 'safe' place to raise issues related to the course for all the students regardless of their gender, religion or culture. The course material, resources and the teaching environment must be accessible for all. In this chapter we indicate some of the important issues to be considered and suggest ways for SGT tutors to adapt their teaching and so ensure that their classes are inclusive and productive for their students.

The chapter gives specific attention to the needs of the following groups of students in SGT:

- multidisciplinary and mixed ability groups
- international students and students for whom English is not a first language
- mature and returning students and 'new learners' (e.g. entering FE and HE through access routes and foundation degree programmes)
- disabled students (e.g. those with impairments such as dyslexia, a hearing or a sight deficiency).

However, the chapter also intends to address the needs of the tutor who is asked to lead a tutorial for a very mixed group of students. How can an interactive class take place when the students have very different starting points in terms of their prior learning and experience, their cultural norms and their abilities and confidence to express themselves in class.

SUPPORTING STUDENTS WORKING IN MULTIDISCIPLINARY AND MIXED ABILITY GROUPS

For many small group tutors the reality of their experience is that the groups they tutor are very mixed in terms of the background experience, abilities and subject specialisms of their students. All small groups are mixed, but some are more mixed than others. This may be a specific feature of course design; for example, in engineering multidisciplinary team projects are organized to provide students with the experience of working across engineering disciplinary boundaries in preparation for the likely reality of their postgraduation employment. For physiotherapy students, part of their course may be run jointly with the medical or social work programmes, again to mimic the working environment that they are preparing to enter.

In other courses, the variations in pre-course entry requirements are a contributory factor in creating diversity. In a business studies degree the first-year students may have studied economics at A level while others may not have studied this subject before starting their university or college course. For physicists the mathematical background of first-year students can be very variable, while the language skills of modern language students can range from a low A level pass to absolute fluency.

Some disciplines and courses are more attractive to mature, returning students. For example, social work programmes attract a number of mature students who have a great diversity of relevant work experience but who may be returning to university or who may not have previous experience of HE.

Whether the diversity in experience and abilities is planned for or a result of local circumstances, the impact on the tutor is very real. In a group of students where some have more knowledge, more confidence and more relevant experience, it can be very difficult to create an environment of positive sharing. It can also be difficult to give explanations and design learning tasks that contribute to the learning of all the students.

151

The tutor needs to be aware and sensitive to the diverse needs of the group members and attempt to acknowledge and support the range of contributions that different students can make. Here we suggest some practical ways in which the tutor may seek to achieve this balance.

Benefit from the differences

In discussion or problem-solving classes it can sometimes be helpful to explicitly mix the class so that you invite students who have a more advanced level of understanding and/or greater experience to share their knowledge and work with students who are more novice. In this way a tutor can explicitly encourage peer support. This does need to be handled with care and consideration and viewed from the perspective of both groups of students. If the more experienced student (acting as a 'student tutor') is not to feel 'used' the benefits of trying to explain things to a colleague and of testing their own understanding, may need to be emphasized by the tutor. If the 'peer-tutored' student isn't to feel undermined and patronized, their contributions need to be given time and attention elsewhere in the class and if possible the roles reversed for different topics.

Differences may also add to the richness of a debate or discussion. If students can be asked to contribute from their different positions and viewpoints, for example, by mixing the views of those who have a more practice based experience with those who have a purely academic stance, a greater appreciation of the whole can be gained. However, the tutor should be sensitive to the possibility that students (and tutors) may not appear to value contributions based on observations of practice as highly as those based on readings and scholarly activity.

There may also be perceived differences in 'status' and very real differences in confidence between group members. This is reported by tutors of multidisciplinary SGT sessions for medical and nursing students. The tutor can specifically ask nursing students and medical students to work together on clinical case studies to better appreciate their corresponding roles in patient care. However, it may be beneficial to closely manage such exchanges to, for example, specifically invite feedback from both the nursing and medical students to avoid any one voice dominating.

Working in cognate groups

To enable students to work in depth and in detail, on particular topics or issues, the tutor may organize specialist or discipline-based subgroups within the SGT session.

Progressive tasks

In both quantitative and qualitative SGT classes it can be very useful to develop learning tasks and activities which have in-built progression. In maths, problems can be set at a novice, intermediate and advanced level and students asked to work through the questions getting as far as they can in the allocated time. Alternatively, students can select their own starting point (i.e. allow more able or experienced students to begin working at a higher level from the outset). Working with new lecturers in HE this approach of group self-selection and self-evaluation can be very helpful in the initial establishment of working groups. In this case the learning task for participants is to give a short, videoed, teaching presentation to a small group of peers. Participants were invited to form a line across the room and to position themselves according to their level of confidence and experience in presenting. They are then asked to form working groups with the people standing next to them in the line and thus share a similar self-diagnosis. The course tutor can then modify his or her approach and pitch the input, feedback and guidance so as to be more demanding for the experienced, confident presenters and more encouraging and supportive for those who are more anxious and new to presenting.

The harmonizing of groups in this way encourages participants in the less experienced group to be very much more relaxed and able to ask questions and raise concerns. Those in the experienced groups are also able to work at an appropriate pace and level that better suits their needs.

SUPPORTING INTERNATIONAL STUDENTS AND STUDENTS FOR WHOM ENGLISH IS NOT A FIRST LANGUAGE

The classrooms of today's universities and colleges are truly global and tutors need to work to accommodate, support and benefit from the diverse and multicultural nature of SGT sessions.

Working in English can provide some international students with an extra level of complexity when they try to take a full and active role in SGT sessions. English has a very large vocabulary, spellings often differ from pronunciation and there is a huge variation in the intonation and annunciation of speakers with different national and international accents. We are asking a lot of our students.

International students are just as individualistic as home students and yet it is possible to see similarities between the situations faced by students from the same part of the world. When considering the specific difficulties faced by non-native speakers this can verge on stereotyping (for which we apologize if we fall into this trap).

Some students have more ability and confidence in reading and writing English than in speaking it. For example, we have observed that students from China often show more advanced writing skills and are more insecure in their verbal skills. Some students may have much better verbal skills and it is the writing (particularly writing 'academic English') that causes the greater problem. Many non-native speakers need more time to read documents and to complete tasks and exercises in class. It is also highly likely that some international students may be much less confident in discussion classes. This may not just be the impact of language difficulties but the affect of cultural differences. In some countries education is delivered by professors in a very didactic way and the opportunities for exchange and dialogue are very limited or completely absent.

However, the reverse may be true. Students who have experience of educational cultures which make extensive use of the oral tradition and who have been strongly encouraged to debate and argue points with their teachers, may appear very confident and even a little abrasive or dominating when compared with other students. For example, students from the United States often appear very confident in class.

What can the teacher do?

There are three basic approaches that a tutor can adopt when working with international students:

- *Referral:* direct the student to a specialist support unit at the university, for example a language centre or bureau for overseas students.
- *One-to-one support:* the tutor can work with the student individually and give extra support, for example when giving

feedback on written work. In some universities 'language mentors' are provided to carry out this role.

■ *Adapting teaching:* the tutor can develop teaching approaches which will have a positive affect on the learning of the international students in the class (and probably on the 'home' students too).

Here we focus on the third approach and in so doing we will draw upon advice and guidance provided by Neil Maclean, from the Language Centre at the London School of Economics (LSE), and upon additional comments provided by Jordi Vaquer-Fanes, from the International Relations Department, also at LSE.

For the tutor there are four potentially problematic issues to be considered in planning SGT sessions attended by international students and non-native speakers of English.

Being as clear as possible

To be as clear as possible it is likely that tutors will need to speak more loudly, slowly and in shorter sentences than they may otherwise do. Care also needs to be taken in the choice of language and terminology chosen. Trying to avoid colloquial terms, acronyms or jargon probably benefits all students but particularly non-native speakers. Tutors should try to organize and structure their explanations and avoid going off the track and rambling about unnecessary anecdotes and stories. When referring to a particular person or an important source it is helpful if tutors write the names or details up on the board or flip chart. Alternatively the tutors can provide such information in a brief handout that the students can refer to and annotate during class. The teaching strategies discussed earlier (Chapters 4 and 6) which aim to give students 'comfortable' thinking and preparation time before asking them to speak in front of the whole group, are particularly helpful for non-native speakers. For example, the use of pair work and preparatory writing tasks can be very helpful.

Checking that the students have understood the tutor

Probably the best way of checking that the students have followed and understood the tutor is to design and set follow-up tasks or exercises that require the students to apply their new understanding. This is not always appropriate, and alternatively pair work can be used. The tutor could explain something and then ask students to re-present the explanation to a partner, or interview their partner about the implications or consequences of the points explained. The tutor could sensitively ask questions of the class by giving pairs or mini-groups of students a short quiz or problem set to work through and thus test their own understanding. Some tutors ask the students to help them in writing up a summary on the board towards the end of the class and use this to check that the students have understood the key issues.

Encouraging students to participate and communicate effectively

Being sensitive to the potential barriers and insecurities felt by international students and trying to provide a class environment where it is OK to get it wrong will particularly help the less confident speakers in the group. The need to give students thinking and planning time before asking them to speak should be planned for by the tutor in the design and implementation of class exercises. Complex tasks should be written down in a handout. It may also be especially helpful to provide additional feedback in class and on written assignments. It is not suggested that SGT tutors should become language teachers but that they can helpfully direct their students to specific sources of help (e.g. study skills information web sites, language support and the assessment criteria) and reinforce the need to develop language skills within the academic discipline.

Ensuring that students have understood each other

In a multicultural classroom English is spoken in a variety of ways and with a diverse range of accents. Tutors may fear that their students do not always follow and understand the contributions made by their classmates. Encouraging speaking students to talk loudly enough for all to hear properly and to manage group discussions so that only one person talks at once are perhaps obvious but important points. Again, writing up difficult words, names, references on the board for the student can help the class. When supporting a struggling speaker, it is important to be patient and resist the urge to finish his or her sentences. However, if students are clearly getting upset about talking in front of the group, don't panic and try to force them to speak by directing questions at them in front of everybody. Gently encourage, address questions towards pairs of students and be appreciative of the contributions and the greater efforts made by shy or under-confident students.

If a contribution is very unclear, the tutor may ask for clarification (sensitively) or check their own understanding by paraphrasing the points presented back to the student in the form of a question (e.g. 'So if I understood you correctly, you are saying that . . .'). It may also be helpful if the tutor can work with the class to produce a clear final summary of the main points, particularly if the debate has been complex and some of the contributions have been difficult to follow. The thoughtfulness of the tutor when trying to accommodate the diverse needs of international students and non-native speakers is likely to benefit all the students in the SGT session.

SUPPORTING MATURE AND RETURNING STUDENTS AND 'NEW LEARNERS'

Mature students are those people who enter university or college education over the age of 21. The UK government has a widening participation agenda and the vision of drawing 50 per cent of 18- to 30-year-olds into HE by 2010. As part of that expansion the UK government has supported the development of a wide range of access routes to HE and FE to encourage a greater and more representative proportion of the population to take part in further and higher education (Higher Education Funding Council for England) (HEFCE 2001). For example, foundation degrees are aimed at students not attracted to traditional higher education and were introduced in September 2001.

Foundation degrees

The UK Department of Education initially made £5 million available to partnerships with approved plans to develop foundation courses. The money was distributed by HEFCE. The foundation courses are sub-degree qualifications that take two years to complete. Many foundation degrees are being offered by local partnerships between FE and HE institutions and it is intended that they can provide a stepping stone between further and higher education for more students (http://www.foundationdegree.org.uk).

157

As a result of initiatives such as the foundation degree and longer standing access programmes, more non-traditional students are now entering higher education. They may well be the first people from their families who have gone to university and are breaking moulds of expectations in doing so. They may have performed poorly in earlier school exams and be very unsure about their abilities and potential.

The needs of this group of 'new learners' are considered here as the issues of low confidence, different expectations and feelings of 'difference'. These feelings of isolation can be shared with some mature students. However, it is clear that there are significant differences between the two groupings too. Mature students are likely to have had a broader life and work, experience to draw upon and many mature students have a more complex set of family commitments to manage and support.

Please forgive the fall into stereotyping. The general trends are being discussed here and not the needs of particular students. We do not intend to pejoratively categorize the needs of individual students but to increase the awareness of new teachers of the diversity of students in today's colleges and universities.

In what ways might mature students differ from other students?

Mature students, as a group, are as varied in their concerns and approaches to study as other groups of students; however, a SGT tutor may wish to pay particular attention to particular traits that older students may show. For example, Roberts (1994) described a number of disruptive tutee behaviours that may block collaborative learning and be problematic for tutors. One particular behaviour, *over-enthusiasm*, is particularly associated with mature students and describes learners who have very high expectations and who have very wide interests but who feel time pressures and put high demands on themselves. Such students may also have longer-range goals and be less preoccupied with immediate tasks. The last point can be very relevant to mature students who have opted to return to studying after a period away from formal education and are likely to have very well-considered and thought-through motivations and goals connected with their university course.

Many mature students will hold positions of responsibility and have high status in other spheres of their lives (Falchikov 2001). They may be mothers or fathers and run a home and household, they may have varied experience of employment, past and present, and hold positions of authority within their communities. Then in a SGT session the tutor may ask them to undertake a very different student role that could involve them in, for example, role-playing, presenting or learning from a fellow student, activities that indicate a very different set of hierarchies and power relationships. Some mature students may find it difficult to cope well with the status inconsistencies that this presents.

> Mature students with families may become stressed by all the conflicting demands on them. They may feel envious of younger students, who only have themselves to worry about, and they may feel that academic staff are oblivious to their other commitments.
>
> Relationships with partners, family and friends can come under strain because of their new life, associates and interests. Some mature students return to education with some bad memories of their previous educational experiences, and they may be doubting their academic abilities. Those who come into HE from access courses, where they received a lot of support, may find University courses unnervingly formal and staff a bit distant.
>
> (University of Huddersfield Counselling service, http://
> www.hud.ac.uk/stu_svc/counselling/dif_students.htm)

Ways to support mature learners

SGT tutors may be younger and, in many ways, less experienced than the mature students in their classes. However, the tutor is likely to have particular expert knowledge and professional skills that the mature student has returned to university to study and learn.

Returning students are frequently very able in particular areas of the curriculum due to their greater work and life experience; however, it may be a long time since they have had to write an essay or present an academic argument in a class debate. Therefore, a tutor should not be surprised if a mature student initially shows a very mixed level of performance. For example, when working with a mature student, a tutor may need to provide advice and guidance on basic study skills and essay writing technique and later with the same student be asked to answer very complex and carefully considered questions.

To avoid feeling 'threatened' and to fully benefit from the presence of mature students in the class, new tutors should

- have confidence in their own knowledge, skills and abilities
- recognize and value the experience of mature students
- be aware and sensitive to the external pressures faced by

some mature students (in allocating work partners for example)

■ acknowledge the long-term goals and motivations of mature students but reinforce the need to meet immediate deadlines and achieve short-term assignments.

A note about 'andragogy'

Knowles (1990 [1973]) developed a theory of adult learning or 'andragogy' (as opposed to pedagogy) with mature learners in mind. Key points being that adult learners need to know why they need to learn something and that the relevance is important and needs to be made very clear. Learning experientially and through problem solving is key to success and viewing the adult learner as self-directed and able to take responsibility is also central to andragogy. For more on a comparison of pedagogy and andragogy see Cross (1981, 1999) and Falchikov (2001).

Principles arising from adult learning theory:

■ Adults need to be involved in the planning and evaluation of their instruction.

■ Experience (including mistakes) provides the basis for learning activities.

■ Adults are most interested in learning subjects that have immediate relevance to their job or personal life.

■ Adult learning is problem-centred rather than content-oriented.

(http://tip.psychology.org/knowles.html)

A number of universities and colleges have invested in the provision of specialist support for the growing numbers of mature students they are seeking to attract back to higher education over the next decade. Advisers and counselling services for mature students are now frequently available. Guidance given on managing work load and study skills can be particularly beneficial. A SGT tutor who feels that a mature student in the group is having particular difficulties in settling into university life or coping with the work should seek additional help and refer the student to specialist departmental and university services for mature students.

Advice given to mature students attending seminars

- Do not wait for others to speak out: the tutor may be relying on you to get the ball rolling.
- Your past experience and study will enrich seminars, so use it as it becomes relevant.
- If you are concerned about saying too much and taking over your seminar group, discuss this with your tutor rather than keeping quiet.
- Your fellow students will not view you as different from them as long as you respect their views and join in as their equal.
- If you have not had a chance to prepare well for a seminar, avoid the temptation to miss it: you will still have something to contribute.

(Lucinda Becker, http://www.palgrave.com/
skills4study/html/mature/matureseminars.htm)

Many small group tutors who have a number of mature students in their classes comment on the 'richness' that these students can bring to discussions and debates. Their additional 'life experience' is a valuable resource for the whole group and sensitive tutors seek to harness this. By recognizing and drawing upon the prior learning and experience of mature students, their presence can very much add to the value of small group teaching.

SUPPORTING DISABLED STUDENTS

From September 2002, the Disability Discrimination Act (DDA) 1995 (as amended by the Special Educational Needs and Disability Act (SENDA) 2001) made it unlawful for providers of education and related services to discriminate against disabled people. The Disability Rights Commission (DRC) is an independent body that has been active in providing guidance on the rights of disabled people and good practice for employers. The advice given below draws upon the clear information that the DRC has provided.

The legal position

In law the college or university is responsible for the actions of

- full-time and part-time employees of the institution in the course of their employment
- external and visiting speakers and others.

However, individual teachers and tutors may also be held responsible for aiding an unlawful act if they knowingly discriminate against a disabled student.

The Act uses a wide definition of disabled person and institutions are expected to take reasonable steps to find out if a person is disabled. It can include people with

- physical or mobility impairments
- visual and hearing impairments
- dyslexia and dyspraxia
- medical conditions
- mental health difficulties.

There are two ways that a tutor could discriminate against a disabled student:

- treating them 'less favourably' than other people
- failing to make a 'reasonable adjustment' when, because of their disability, they are placed at a 'substantial disadvantage' when compared to other students.

The Act applies to all the activities and facilities institutions provide wholly or mainly for students, including, for example:

- all aspects of teaching and learning, including SGT, lectures, lab work, practicals, field trips, etc.
- e-learning, distance learning and teaching resources
- examinations and assessments
- learning resources, including libraries, computer facilities, etc.

From the SGT tutor's point of view the main focus of the legislation is the clear need to make *anticipatory reasonable adjustments* to the teaching, learning and assessment approaches used in order to make the learning experience accessible to all students.

Exactly what might constitute a reasonable adjustment will depend on the needs of the students, the requirements and academic standards of the course, the resources of the institution and the practicality of the adjustment (including its impact on other students). In general terms a reasonable adjustment might be any action that helps to alleviate a substantial disadvantage, for example:

- changing institutional procedures
- adapting the curriculum, electronic or other materials, or modifying the delivery of teaching
- providing additional services, such as a sign language interpreter or materials in large font or Braille
- raising the awareness and training staff to work with disabled people
- making modifications to the physical environment.

'Anticipatory' adjustments means that universities (and teachers) should consider what adjustments future disabled students may need, and make them in advance. The QAA (1999) *Code of Practice for Students with Disabilities* recommends a series of adaptations, as outlined here:

Precept 10
The delivery of programmes should take into account the needs of disabled people, or, where appropriate, be adapted to accommodate their individual requirements.

Institutions should consider making arrangements which ensure that all academic staff and technical staff:

- plan and employ teaching and learning strategies which make the delivery of the programme as inclusive as possible;
- know and understand the learning implications of any disabilities of the student whom they teach and are responsive to student feedback;
- make individual adaptations to delivery that are appropriate for particular students.

(QAA 1999)

The Disability Rights Commission (DRC) offers a conciliation service for students and institutions to reconcile any differences informally. If both parties do not agree to conciliation, or if conciliation fails, a student or applicant can take a case to a county court (in England or Wales) or a sheriff court (in Scotland).

Confidentiality

Universities are expected to take reasonable steps to find out about a student's disability. Once the university is aware that a student has a disability, because either it is obvious (e.g. visible) or the student has disclosed it, the institution has a responsibility not to discriminate. It is worth remembering that if a student tells his or her tutor that he or she has a disability then, in the eyes of the law, the student has informed the university.

Students do, of course, have a right to confidentiality, through the Data Protection Act, and separately within the Disability Discrimination Act. However, for some courses there may be particular health and safety requirements that means disabled students are required to disclose certain disabilities for the safety of themselves and others.

Tutors: making reasonable adaptations

Individual needs

If you are aware that any students in your class have a disability, arrange to speak with them tactfully to discuss their needs at the earliest opportunity. Try not to make global assumptions about their disability: the student will be the expert on his or her own condition and situation. Discuss the needs of the students with them in order to better understand their position and ask for their advice on how you can support their learning and help them to fully participate in your class.

If you would like to find out more about a particular kind of disability or better understand a particular disabling condition, there is a list of information web sites, which you may find useful, at the end of this chapter in Table 10.1.

Anticipatory adjustments

Tutors can help to ensure that disabled students are not substantially disadvantaged by some very simple adaptations to their teaching practice in seminars, problems classes and seminars.

- Are teaching rooms allocated and timetabled with the needs of disabled students in mind? (Physical access, lighting and acoustics may be relevant issues to consider.)
- Do tutors face the front when they speak, especially when

they are using PowerPoint presentations or writing on a board?

■ Do teachers provide handouts in advance and online?

■ Do tutors use microphones or allow taping of classes where this would assist students?

■ Do teachers read out material presented visually to support those unable to see?

■ Are students with communication difficulties, or those who may find seminar presentations difficult for other reasons, supported when preparing their talks?

■ Do tutors work to ensure that only one person speaks at a time during debates and discussions?

Adaptations for group working

Some adjustments may be necessary to ensure that disabled students can fully contribute to and benefit from group based learning.

■ Are students supported to ensure that all group members can fully participate and be involved in the group?

■ Do tutors talk through with groups any practical difficulties that might arise from having a diverse group, and make sure any appropriate adjustments can be made?

■ Where group work is assessed, are adjustments made to ensure that every student's contribution can be measured? Even if learning outcomes need to be measured and assessed differently.

Teaching resources and online tutorials

Access to learning resources is essential for all students and so the design and distribution of materials and learning facilities needs to be undertaken with inclusivity in mind.

■ Are videos and other audio materials provided with subtitles, interpretation or transcripts?

■ Are paper-based materials provided in advance for reading or presented in Braille, large print or online?

■ Are booklists provided sufficiently in advance for a student to obtain texts on tape or in Braille?

- Are electronic materials fully accessible? Can those using supportive technology (such as screen-reading software) access them?
- Is the layout and structure of virtual learning environments suitable for students with dyslexia or with partial sight?
- Do sound clips have text alternatives or subtitles?
- Does the software allow students to go at their own speed or take rest breaks?

(Adapted from guidance provided by the Disability Rights Commission, http://www.drc-gb.org)

POSITIVE IMPACT

In today's universities SGT tutors are likely to have a very mixed and diverse group of students in their classes. Teachers who work to respond to the needs of individual students (whether they have language difficulties or disabilities etc.) often find that their efforts are doubly rewarded because the changes they make in their teaching have a positive impact for all their students.

Being prepared in advance and having materials available on the web for students to download before the class helps everyone. Talking clearly and presenting thoughtfully does too. Using teaching techniques that give 'comfortable' thinking time and encourage the full involvement of all are supportive of those who have communication difficulties, but are likely to result in a higher quality of contributions being offered by all students.

It is suggested that tutors make their willingness to support students who have a disability very explicit when meeting a new group of students and clearly invite students to work with them to maximize their ability to work effectively in the SGT session.

CONCLUDING REMARKS

The diversity of the student population is often seen as a problem for teachers and much that is written is posed in terms of 'difficulties' and 'problems' to be overcome. As we have seen in this chapter, there are additional things to think about in conducting a small group teaching session for a varied mix of students but it also provides a rich resource for staff and students to draw upon in discussion. Having people take part in debates who have very different life experiences, backgrounds,

TABLE 10.1 Additional sources of information on specific disabilities and support organizations

Organization	Web site
Action for M.E. (myalgic encephalomyelitis or Chronic Fatigue Syndrome)	www.afme.org.uk
Association for Spina Bifida and Hydrocephalus (ASBAH)	www.asbah.org.uk
British Council of Disabled People	www.bcodp.org.uk
British Dyslexia Association	www.bda-dyslexia.org.uk
Dyspraxia Foundation	www.emmbrook.demon.co.uk/dysprax/what.htm
Epilepsy Action	www.epilepsy.org.uk
Mental Health Foundation	www.mentalhealth.org.uk
MIND (For better mental health)	www.mind.org.uk
National Autistic Society	www.nas.org.uk
OASIS (Online Asperger's Syndrome Information Resources)	www.udel.edu/bkirby/asperger/index.html
Royal National Institute for Deaf People	www.rnid.org.uk
Royal National Institute for the Blind	www.rnib.org.uk
SKILL: National Bureau for Students with Disabilities	www.skill.org.uk
TechDis (For information on making electronic materials accessible)	www.techdis.ac.uk
University Students with Autism and Asperger's Syndrome	www.users.dircon.co.uk/~cns/index.html

beliefs and expectations can broaden and deepen debate and very much enrich the learning experience of all who take part, including the teacher. The challenge for all teachers is to make more of the benefits than the difficulties and to provide a welcoming and stimulating environment for all the students who come to class.

FURTHER READING

HEFCE (2001) *Strategies for Widening Participation in Higher Education*, Guide 01/30, http://www.hefce.ac.uk/pubs/hefce/2001/01_36.htm (accessed 9 June 2003).

QAA (1999) *Code of Practice for the Assurance of Academic Quality and Standards in Higher Education: Students with Disabilities*, http://www.qaa.ac.uk/public/COP/COPswd/contents.htm (accessed 12 June 2003).

Waterfield, J. and West, B. (2002) *SENDA Compliance in Higher Education*, South West Academic Network for Disability Support (SWANDS), University of Plymouth and HEFCE.

USEFUL WEB SITES

http://www.drc-gb.org Disabilities Rights Commission. For general information on disabilities and disabilities legislation (accessed 9 June 2003).

http://www.plymouth.ac.uk/disability Disability ASSIST services, University of Plymouth. For advice on making the curriculum accessible to disabled students (accessed 9 June 2003).

http://www.dmu.ac.uk/services/student_services/slas/dyslexia/inform_staff.jsp?ComponentID=5757&SourcePageID=5755#1 De Montfort University, Leicester, web pages giving guidance to staff on supporting dyslexic students (accessed 9 June 2003).

http://www.foundationdegree.org.uk/ Department for Education and Skills foundation degree web site (accessed 9 June 2003).

http://www.kingston.ac.uk/LTDU/dysstaff.htm Kingston University's formal Dyslexia Policy document and good guidelines on marking (accessed 9 June 2003).

http://www.niace.org.uk/ NIACE's (National Institute for Adult Continuing Education) web site provides information, policy discussions and links to other organizations concerned with adult learning and supporting older learners (accessed 9 June 2003).

http://www.lifelonglearning.co.uk/ This web site seeks to encourage, promote and develop lifelong learning and is supported by the Department for Education and Skills (accessed 9 June 2003).

Chapter 11

Assessing students working in SGT sessions

INTRODUCTION

The assessment of students and their work is a huge topic in itself and covered in other books in this series. However, the separation of 'helping students to learn' (teaching and learning approaches) and 'finding out if they have learnt' (assessment) is clearly false and can be an unhelpful notion in course design. When considering assessment in the SGT setting, many of the generic 'key issues' of assessment are relevant. What are the purposes of the assessment? Is the assessment summative (i.e. counts for marks and grades) or is it formative (i.e. to give constructive feedback to the learner)? What aspects of knowledge attainment, skills and attitudinal development can or should be assessed? And what methods can make this process reliable, valid and fair for the students while being manageable, resourceable and effective from the tutor's perspective?

In this chapter we review the most commonly found forms of assessment associated with SGT and give examples of how they are working in practice in a range of disciplines. These approaches are summarized in Table 11.1. The list is not intended to be comprehensive but to indicate the forms of assessments that the part-time or occasional tutor may well be asked to undertake.

(Please see Haines (2004) for a full discussion of the practicalities of assessing student's written work and much more on the fundamentals of course assessment.)

■ **TABLE 11.1** Common forms of assessments associated with SGT and potential assessors

Mode of work	Possible method(s) of assessment	Who can assess?
Written work	Mini-projects, assignments, essays, etc.	T, P and S
Contribution to class discussions and class work	Preparatory notes, recorded observations, reflective log, contribution record, etc.	T, P and S
Presentation and oral communication skills	Giving a short presentation to the class and taking questions	T, P and S
Team or group working	Group projects or group presentations	T, P and S
Continuing personal, academic and professional development	Portfolio, reflective log, journal of critical incidents	T and S
	Links with student profiles or records of achievement	T and S

Key: T = tutor, P = peers, S = student

POSSIBLE ASSESSORS: TUTOR, PEERS AND STUDENTS

In Table 11.1 it is suggested that for most forms of assessment used in the SGT context, it is possible to use self and peer assessment as part of the process. Many tutors find the use of formative self and/or peer assessment in a tutorial or seminar to be a strong aid to learning. Putting the students themselves in the shoes of the assessor and asking them to judge the quality of their work, or that of their colleagues, increases awareness and understanding of the assessment criteria. When viewed from the assessor's perspective the strengths and weaknesses of the work can often be seen more clearly.

> It has been shown that good formative assessment practices can lead to greater learning gain than almost any other educational innovation.
>
> (Knight 2002)

Boud *et al.* (2001) present six features that need to be taken into account when designing assessment strategies that support peer learning

 170

■ **TABLE 11.2** Designing assessment to support peer learning

Assessment features	Issues to address
Focus on learning outcomes	Focusing on the central learning outcomes, whether they be knowledge attainment, skills or self-development, will lead to the adoption of fundamentally different assessment processes.
Holistic design	Focus on the whole assessment experience of the learner, seeking to integrate peer learning assessment and to combat the tendency that SGT assessment is marginalized and/or undermined by other, more predominant, forms of assessments used on the course.
Consequences on student learning	Does the assessment encourage deep and meaningful approaches to study?
Contribution to lifelong learning	Does the assessment encourage a learner to move from dependence and independence towards interdependence and professionalism, i.e. does the assessment value collaborative learning and professional development?
Use of appropriate emphasis and language	Communications about the assessment methods and criteria are clear and commonly understood by all. The assessment emphasis is on feedback and development rather than on ranking and competition.
Promoting critical reflection	SGT encourages critical reflection and the skills to clearly express oneself. The assessment should ideally not cut across these benefits and encourage reciprocal communication and willingness to give and receive feedback.

(summarized in Table 11.2). These are drawn from Boud's (1995) paper that discusses assessment practices that are in alignment with the learning outcomes for the course, i.e. practices that encourage the students to learn what you wanted and intended them to learn.

The uncomfortable compromise

At the heart of the six value statements in Table 11.2 is the difficulty that if all we assess in our students is their ability to achieve learning independently, they will have less incentive to co-operate and work collaboratively in class. If we could but design assessments that pull in the same direction and explicitly value the peer learning and group-based activities of SGT, then we will directly appeal to the strategic learning approach adopted by many HE students. If we assess it, we communicate that we value it, and many students will respond to that message.

This may be seen as a somewhat cynical approach but students use our assessment choices to help them prioritize and manage their work effort (a professional skill?). Therefore, if we really value the skills developed in SGT and collaborative working, we should do so in our assessment design.

That said, it is not always easy or cost-effective to try to measure every complex skill that a student can develop in SGT. It is always more difficult to accurately assess a *process* compared with a *product*. In many universities there is a requirement that any process, such as a student's oral presentation, should be judged by more than one assessor to increase the *reliability* of the marking. Tutors may also wish to video sample their students' presentations so that they can be viewed by the external examiner for the course in order to monitor and check the standards of assessment. This increases the cost of assessment.

We may also struggle to ensure that our assessments are *valid* when we seek to assess such processes as, for example, teamworking. Often what we end up assessing is how much each student has contributed to the team in terms of time and effort and/or the quality of the end product that the teams have produced or presented. Both of these measures do not actually assess teamworking. One student may have had a limited but dramatic impact on the team's effectiveness and success while in another group one student may have produced the end product virtually on their own. So more complex assessment methods are needed to really assess group working and the skills of collaboration and teamwork. It may sometimes be impossible to develop an assessment method that can achieve an acceptable degree of reliability and validity and remain manageable by both staff and students. The complexity, the investment for both the tutor and students may make the price too costly for high stakes, high value, summative assessment.

Many module or course designers thus find themselves attaching a relatively small weighting to SGT, collaborative learning, assessments. Course designers try to maximize the benefits and minimize the difficulties. By making SGT assessments count in terms of marks and exam results (so as to encourage the students to participate fully in SGT) but not so much that they have a serious impact on any student's individual degree classification (because of worries about reliability, validity and fairness).

This is not an altogether comfortable compromise and the emphasis that the Dearing report (1997) placed on the development of key skills may require course designers to review their approach. Specifically, to find ways of increasing the assessment weighting of SGT activities, particularly those associated with the collaborative working and the development of cognitive and key skills.

We now move on to focus on the immediate concerns of tutors who have been asked to assess their students engaged in SGT activities. What learning outcomes are to be assessed and what methods of assessment can be used?

ASSESSING STUDENTS IN SGT ACTIVITIES

The five aspects of student work in SGT to be discussed are:

- assessing written work
- assessing contribution to class discussions and class work
- assessing presentation and oral communication skills
- assessing team or group working
- assessing continuing personal, academic and professional development.

Assessing written work

This is a huge topic in its own right and is therefore the subject of another book in this series (Haines 2004). Haines provides guidance on marking work fairly, coping with the assessment of large classes, dealing with plagiarism and on giving constructive feedback to the students.

Assessing contribution to class discussions and class work

The following is an example of information provided for students who are taking a history module in which 10 per cent of the module marks are awarded on the basis of attendance and contribution to the seminar:

173

The criteria for assessing the 10 per cent of the course-work awarded for attendance at and contribution to seminars are participation in discussion, and the depth of knowledge, coherence of argument and clarity of expression displayed. The quality of the paper which every student is required to present to one seminar is also taken into account.

Such course information is not atypical and demonstrates that weightings are frequently low for the assessment of contribution (usually between 5 and 15 per cent) and that assessment criteria can be difficult to express with absolute clarity.

The motivations for wishing to assess students' contribution to class work and class discussions are summarized here:

- to encourage everyone to prepare for class
- to encourage everyone to develop their communication skills
- to encourage class interaction in order to deepen and broaden discussion and learning
- to discourage 'free-riders'.

However, there are undoubtedly several disadvantages in trying to assess contribution to class work:

- assessment may inhibit the discussion
- students may find attending the class more stressful
- students may be detrimentally affected by external factors outside their control (e.g. the dynamics of the class)
- differences in culture, background, gender and language may inhibit some from participating fully.

And from the tutor's point of view:

- 'contribution' can be difficult to assess reliably and objectively
- assessment criteria are difficult to describe clearly
- assessment adds to the tutor's responsibilities and role when the tutor already has lots to think about.

EXAMPLE OF COURSE INFORMATION
Assessing 'Contribution to tutorials' in a politics course

There are two major factors that go into the assessment of your contribution to tutorials: the quality of preparation and relevance of the contribution you make each week and the regularity of your attendance. As an example, one unexcused absence will reduce an otherwise outstanding (= distinction) overall level of contribution to a credit level; three unexcused absences will reduce it to a bare pass mark. Obviously, you make no contribution to tutorials you don't attend. Equally, one should not expect recognition for contributions to a tutorial in which one had little to say.

[If there are valid reasons why you cannot contribute fully or effectively to tutorial discussions, please raise them privately with your tutor at your earliest convenience.]

(http://www.labour.adelaide.edu.au/ssis/politics/
Course_Objectives.97.Mk2.html, accessed 8 June 2003)

This module information clearly asks students to inform their tutor if they have any valid reasons why they may be restricted in their ability to contribute to the tutorial discussions. It is very important to discover if any students suffer from a disabling condition that may inhibit or prevent them from contributing in class, as this could have a detrimental affect on their course work assessments.

Some alternative approaches

As we have seen, tutors want to assess contribution to encourage students to value and work hard in SGT sessions but the assessment of 'contribution' is very difficult to do fairly and reliably so tutors often opt to keep assessment weightings for this low. Here are some alternative strategies that can encourage students to attend and participate fully in class.

- The use of student self-assessment through a structured log and asking the students to monitor their own participation in class work and/or discussions. By asking the students to rate their own contribution to class and identify their own strengths and weaknesses it should be possible to encourage

175

them to see the value of their contributions and participation. Such an approach would need to be preceded by a class discussion of 'What makes for a useful contribution' or 'How can everyone participate in class'. This could also be linked to the development of ground rules as discussed earlier.

■ Make attendance at tutorials, problems classes or seminars compulsory and make attendance at, say, 80 per cent of classes a prerequisite of being entered for the summative assessment, e.g. end of module examination.

■ Rather than trying to assess something as general (and difficult to capture) as 'contribution' or 'participation', require the students to undertake a specific task, or series of tasks, that the tutor can more readily assess in the class. This could include activities such as leading a section of the discussion or giving a presentation (see the following section on 'Assessing presentation and oral communication skills'.)

■ Ask students to hand in or email to you their preparatory notes or worked examples before the class. Alternatively, if you are able to use WebCT or Blackboard (or a similar intranet or internet-based course support system) ask the students to post their preparatory work to the course virtual discussion board. This preparatory work could also be assessed as an integral course-work assessment for the module and encourage students to prepare for class.

Guidelines for assessing student performance in class

Whatever approach is used to assess a student's performance in the class, it may be helpful to consider the following general guidelines:

■ It is often easier for the tutor, and more transparent for the students, to assess performance on a clearly defined task, e.g. a ten-minute talk.

■ Specify clearly the criteria for assessing the performance of students and make these available at the beginning of the module.

■ Provide students with the opportunity to learn and practise skills before they are assessed, e.g. if you intend to use video recordings in the assessment process, use it during practice sessions too.

- Make sure that the assessment is fair to all groups; it should not discriminate against women, different cultural groups, students with disabilities and others.

- Consider how to involve the rest of the class, e.g. in giving peer feedback to the presenter using the same assessment criteria as the tutor.

- If several tutors are leading SGT sessions on the same course, it is important that they are all using the same assessment methods and criteria. It is a very good idea to meet together and share thoughts and agree common practice.

- Be able to evidence your assessment practice for external examiners and quality reviewers, e.g. double marking and peer marking to show reliability and consistency of markers, videoed practice, student handouts, PowerPoint presentations and other practice-generated artefacts.

Assessing presentation and oral communication skills

Many SGT sessions require the students to give short presentations on work that they have prepared. The development of communication skills has been highlighted in the key skills agenda as being important for the future employability of graduates. Therefore, most curricula include opportunities for students to practise and be assessed in giving presentations at several times during their studies. The student's experience should ideally build on what has gone before. For example, a second-year student could be asked to give a longer, more complex presentation, to a larger audience, than a first-year student. In addition to the increased demands and difficulty of the learning task, the assessment criteria used to assess from one level to the next, should also seek to reflect this progression and further develop. For example, first-year students may be assessed in terms of their abilities to speak and explain clearly, to use appropriate visual aids and structure their talk well. Third-year students could be assessed, additionally, on their ability to engage the audience, respond to questions and produce a summary of their talk posted up on the course web site.

Commonly students are asked to prepare a ten-minute presentation to give to the next class. The use of audio-visual aids, such as the board, overhead projector or PowerPoint presentation software, may be encouraged. Students may also be expected to produce a short handout for their peers in which they can summarize their key points, raise questions and provide reference details. By asking students to produce a handout for their presentation, they are not only producing a useful document for their peers but also generating a 'product' that can be used to assess the 'content' of their talk. The assessment of the presentation can then be focused more directly on the assessment of presentation skills. This clarifies and simplifies the role of assessors and makes the use of peer assessment more attractive, because much research has shown that students are just as capable of judging presentation skills reliably as their tutors.

Beyond the seminar presentation: a broader view of oral communication skills

In some disciplines the presenting student may also be asked to lead the class discussion following his or her talk. The tutor may also be interested in assessing the student's ability to manage the discussion.

In disciplines such as medicine, the tutor may wish to assess how a student interviews and takes a patient's history or is able to communicate difficult news.

In engineering, architecture or design it may be appropriate to judge how well a student can consult with a potential client in order to establish a clear brief and produce an attractive business proposal.

In international or industrial relations it is likely to be important that students are able to understand the process and develop the skills of negotiation.

In concentrating on the specific 'communication skills' learning outcomes in SGT, appropriate assessment criteria can be agreed. One way that this can be achieved is to start by considering the common errors that occur in the form of communication you wish to address. What mistakes do people often make? Doing this together, as part of the class preparation for the communication task, is likely to help the students see more clearly what is expected of them and help them understand the feedback they may receive from assessors.

As an example, the common errors in communication in a medical consultation are listed here:

- use of jargon
- lack of precision

- avoidance of personal issues
- failure to pick up verbal leads
- unnecessary repetition of questions
- inappropriate questions
- lack of clarification
- lack of control
- non-facilitation
- assumption that there is only one problem
- time management of the consultation.

(adapted from Maguire *et al.* 1986, by Brown *et al.* 1997)

From a common understanding of the difficulties that can occur in a communication process, it is possible to then move on to develop an assessment tool.

A common approach to the assessment of communication, live practice and process is to have a marking sheet which lists aspects of the performance that are important and some kind of rating scale to indicate the level of ability or achievement that is demonstrated by the student. When developing assessment tools it is important to consider the following:

- Identify the qualities that you want students to demonstrate in their performance (are some more important than others?)
- Identify the criteria that you will use to assess whether students have displayed these qualities.
- Draw up an assessment guide which will enable you to record your judgements and give feedback to students.

(http://www.vuw.ac.nz/utdc/documentation/
AssessingParticipation.pdf, accessed 8 June 2003)

Examples of assessment pro-formas

Tables 11.3 and 11.4 are examples of marking sheets for evaluating student presentations.

Assessing team or group working

As with all forms of assessments, it is important to be clear about the purpose of group work assessment. There are many reasons why you may wish to assess students who have engaged in a group activity in the

TABLE 11.3 A marking sheet for evaluating student presentations

Mark / Criteria	1	2	3	4	Total
Organization	Audience cannot understand presentation because there is no sequence of information.	Audience has difficulty following presentation because student jumps around.	Student presents information in logical sequence which audience can follow.	Student presents information in logical, interesting sequence which audience can follow.	
Subject knowledge	Student does not have grasp of information. Student cannot answer questions about subject.	Student is uncomfortable with information and is able to answer only rudimentary questions.	Student is at ease with expected answers to all questions, but fails to elaborate.	Student demonstrates full knowledge (more than required) by answering all class questions with explanations and elaboration.	
Graphics	Student uses superfluous graphics or no graphics.	Student occasionally uses graphics that rarely support text and presentation.	Student's graphics relate to text and presentation.	Student's graphics explain and reinforce screen text and presentation.	
Mechanics	Student's presentation has four or more spelling errors or grammatical errors.	Presentation has three misspellings and/or grammatical errors.	Presentation has no more than two misspellings and/or grammatical errors.	Presentation has no misspellings or grammatical errors.	
Eye contact	Student reads all of report with no eye contact.	Student occasionally uses eye contact, but still reads most of report.	Student maintains eye contact most of the time but frequently returns to notes.	Student maintains eye contact with audience, seldom returning to notes.	
Elocution	Student mumbles, incorrectly pronounces terms, and speaks too quietly for students at the back of class to hear.	Student's voice is low. Student incorrectly pronounces terms. Audience members have difficulty hearing presentation.	Student's voice is clear. Student pronounces most words correctly. Most audience members can hear presentation.	Student uses a clear voice and correct, precise pronunciation of terms so that all audience members can hear presentation.	
				Total points:	

Note: This marking sheet was developed by the Information Technology Evaluation Services, Department of Public Instruction, North Carolina State University, http://www.ncsu.edu/midlink/rub.pres.html

█ TABLE 11.4 Oral presentation marking sheet

Name of presenter:
Date:
Class:

Please indicate, in the grid below, how well you thought the presenter met the presentation criteria, where (1) is a *low* score and (5) is a *high* score.

Criteria	1	2	3	4	5
Content					
Coherence and organization					
Creativity					
Visual aids					
Oral skills					
Audience participation					
Use of time					
Handout quality					
Answering questions					

Please do take a couple of minutes at the end of the presentation to give your colleague some helpful feedback in the comments section below. In practice your comments may be of more immediate use to your colleague in improving their skills than the rating scores above so please be specific and constructive.

One thing the presenter should try to keep doing is:

One thing the presenter should try to stop doing is:

Comments

SGT session, for example to give credit for teamworking skills, to encourage all to participate, to grade the results of group work. Depending on the focus tutors will then need to respond to the four factors determining group work assessment listed here:

■ Whether what is to be assessed is the product of the group work, the process of the group work, or both (and if the latter, what proportion of each)?

- What criteria will be used to assess the aspect(s) of group work of interest (and who will determine these criteria – lecturer, students or both)?
- Who will apply the assessment criteria and determine marks (lecturer, students, peer and/or self-assessment or a combination)?
- How will marks be distributed (shared group mark, group average, individually, combination)?

(Australian Universities Teaching Committee, http://www.cshe.unimelb.edu.au/assessinglearning)

There are four basic assessment approaches that can be used to assess students who are working in groups:

- individual assessment
- same mark allocation
- divided mark allocation
- self-assessment of teamworking skills.

Individual assessment

In individual assessment, the students work together to complete activities and learning tasks but they then produce individual work that will be individually assessed. For example, students may collect information together and discuss their results but they would then write individual reports of their work. Or each group member could be allocated and then be assessed on, a designated section of the teamwork. This strategy avoids the difficulties of dividing group marks but does not encourage true collaboration. Such a method is clearly not appropriate if the tutor wishes to assess the development of teamworking skills but may be relevant if the teamworking has been a vehicle for individual learning.

Same mark allocation

In the same mark allocation approach, the group work together to produce a joint product (e.g. a group report or poster). This is assessed and each group member receives the same share of the group mark. Everybody gets the same grade. The advantages are a reduced marking load for the tutor and a strong incentive for the team to work together for the common good. Some tutors also use the 'real world' argument to endorse this approach, saying that the teams that students belong to in the future, in the workplace, will fail or succeed collectively and thus this assessment method is appropriate where the development of professional skills is a particular learning focus. However, students can feel that weaker or non-participating group members benefit unfairly from the work of their peers and so the 'free-rider' can cause problems for fellow students and the tutor. It may also mean that students who are having difficulties remain hidden from the tutor and do not receive the help they need.

Divided mark allocation

In the divided mark allocation approach, the student group are allocated their joint group assessment but this mark is distributed between the group members on the basis of their different contributions to the team effort. So a student who has put a great deal of effort into the teamwork should obtain higher marks, or the student whose high quality input made a significant different to the teamwork would also attract a higher proportion of the marks.

There are many different mechanisms for dividing up the marks. Students may be asked to assess themselves and their fellow group members, according to their level of contribution, using a criteria based rating sheet which they (openly or secretly) submit to the tutor. The tutor then combines all the group ratings for each group member to determine the individual's overall peer assessment mark and divides the marks accordingly. Table 11.5 shows an example of a peer assessment marking sheet.

Alternatively everyone could be awarded the 'group mark' from the tutor who has assessed the collaboratively produced work. The group mark is then weighted for each student by an individual factor based on each student's own contribution to the group work. The weighting factor is jointly agreed within the group. The tutor usually sets an upper and lower limit such that a student who made an above average contribution can get up to +5 marks, a below average contribution up to −5 marks and an average contribution will get the unmodified group mark. (For further examples of different peer assessment models please see http://learn.lincoln.ac.nz/groupwork/assessment/pa_models.htm, accessed 8 June 2003.)

183

TABLE 11.5 Peer assessment marking sheet

Please indicate the level of contribution you and each of your team members have made in the different aspects of group working given in the assessment sheet below.

In each of the five aspects of teamwork given (criteria) please award a mark of between 0 (for no contribution at all) to a maximum of 20 (for a major or outstanding contribution) for each student in the team. By totalling the columns you can give a '% contribution' mark for each member of the team. Please submit your assessment form to the course tutor who will use the % contribution assessments to fairly weight the team members' final marks.

Criteria	Yourself	Student 1	Student 2	Student 3	Student 4
Leadership and planning 20%					
Group support and management 20%					
Generating results 20%					
Interpreting results 20%					
Writing the report 20%					
Total contribution *100%*					

Consequences of the 'divided mark' strategy

The divided mark approach does help negate the 'free-rider' problem and students perceive it to be fair; however, its complexity no doubt causes an increased workload for the tutor. The process can be strengthened if clear criteria are used and there is a requirement that all student decisions are justifiable and evidenced. This helps to avoid bias and students assessing on the basis of who they like and don't like.

It should also be noted that tutors report that in the majority of cases (approximately nine out of ten groups) the students will opt to give each other equal marks initially. Students will vote to lower the marks of their peers only if they have done absolutely nothing. Student team members will tolerate and reward equally very variable contributions

FIGURE 11.1 When students are doing the marking

to the team effort. So this is a very 'blunt' assessment tool that will be employed only if the students are very fed up with a particular group member, for example if he or she has not turned up for any group meetings (see Figure 11.1).

An alternative assessment mechanism for 'seeing the individual within the team' is for the tutor to give each student a short viva to help him or her gain insight into the extent and the nature of each student's contribution to the group work. This can then be used to moderate the group mark by 5 or 10 per cent. However, this is not appropriate if the numbers of students are large, as the resulting increase in workload becomes an issue.

Self-assessment of teamworking skills

A very different approach to the assessment of group working is based upon the students self-assessing their skills development, performance and participation within the SGT context. Here all the students would be asked to keep a personal diary or a log of their group based activity in order to self-assess their contribution to the team and encourage the development of communication and teamworking skills. This approach is much more comfortably associated with formative, developmental assessment rather than absolute reliable grading. Again there are many different approaches that may be appropriate.

Students can be asked to pre-diagnose their teamworking skills, set themselves developmental goals and then measure their progress against them. Alternatively they could be asked to record and describe their experiences of group working and reflect upon it, considering their own strengths and weaknesses. A third approach might be to ask students to keep a personal diary in order to be able to write a reflective essay at the end of the group working experience. A helpful strategy here is to invite students to use a form of 'critical incident analysis', that is select and describe key incidents in the group working experience and reflect upon them in order to explain to the tutor what they have learnt from the experience.

Some tutors have found it helpful to use diagnostic and self-perception inventories, more commonly used in the analysis of effective business teams, to analyse and interpret group behaviour in their students. Probably the most commonly used model of individual differences in the team context is 'Belbin's Team Roles'. Based upon a study of what makes for an effective team, Belbin (1993) described nine team roles that are needed in the most effective teams. The roles are given in Table 11.6 together with a brief description of the characteristics each displays. Using Belbin's descriptions may also help students to analyse their own ways of working with others.

Questions students could ask themselves

- Am I unique in my team?
- What roles do I contribute to?
- Where are my strengths and weaknesses?
- How much should I seek to restrain my natural style for the good of the team?

TABLE 11.6 Team roles described by Belbin (1993)

Team role	Characteristics
Implementor	Stable and controlled, an organizer, turns ideas into actions, needs stable structures and tries to create them.
Resource investigator	Relaxed and sociable with lots of contacts. Networker, keeps the team in touch with the outside world.
Co-ordinator	Clarifies objectives and sets the agenda. Stable, dominant, extrovert, non-aggressive, social leader.
Shaper	Anxious, dominant leader who shapes the team's efforts. Strategic, visionary, quick to challenge and easily frustrated.
Plant	High IQ, ideas person, original thinker, may be more of a loner, may take criticism badly.
Monitor evaluator	High IQ, introvert, serious, measured, dispassionate analysis, not original. Will check and evaluate. May dampen morale.
Team worker	Most sensitive to team and individual needs. Likeable, popular, loyal, good communicator, negotiator, smoother. Hates confrontation.
Finisher	Anxious, introvert. Dots the 'I's and crosses the 'T's. Maintains sense of urgency, and impatient of inaccuracy or casual approaches. May get bogged down with the detail.
Specialist	High degree of subject expertise, introvert and narrowly focused. Can be a 'law unto themselves'.

- Who am I most different from in the team?
- Who am I most similar to?
- How can I work effectively with others?

The students asked to self-assess and reflect upon their own teamworking may find such tools helpful and give a 'common language' to be able to talk in detail about their role and contribution to the team.

And finally . . .

Whatever method is chosen to assess group work, it is very important that tutors know why they are assessing the students in the way that they are and the students are entirely clear about the method, its details, its rationale, and its justification from the outset.

Assessing continuing personal, academic and professional development

The favoured method for assessing the personal and professional development of an individual is the evidenced portfolio. The portfolio is a collection of evidence and personal reflections presented by the student to show that they have achieved the specified learning outcomes of the course. The portfolio may be prescriptively structured requiring the students to submit specific evidence, e.g. peer evaluation of their seminar presentation together with their own evaluation and reflections on their work. Or the portfolio design can be decided by the students themselves and in some disciplines the forms of evidence can be many and varied, e.g. CD-Roms, links to web sites, videoed practice and so on.

As many students have already experienced keeping 'student profiles' at school, the notion of collecting, collating and presenting evidence of their progress is not alien. However, the emphasis in a developmental portfolio is to capture the 'journey' of development rather than only showcase successes. A developmental portfolio should include examples that may not have been completely successful thus allowing the student to talk about what they learnt from the experience, what they would do differently next time and what they need to work on in their own development of skills etc.

This is likely to be quite different from the experience of producing a student profile in which the student has documented personal achievements and triumphs in order to apply for a university place or a job. The difference between the two approaches would certainly need to be explained and discussed with the students. This is vital if the portfolio is to move beyond being a purely descriptive piece, 'What I did in my class was . . .' and avoid being only a showcase of success, '. . . and the whole class thought my talk was great' to being a tool for self-analysis and progress: 'The introduction worked well, I felt that I got the group's attention, but I was not happy with the way I explained the derivation of the equation, I could see that I had lost some people . . . I think I could have used the board there and . . .'.

One further development of the portfolio is the electronic or web-based portfolio. Being able to present linked and collated electronic resources and evidence, including tutor feedback, essay plans, communications, information pages etc. gives the portfolio extra flexibility and avoids the need to carry heavy A4 files of paper from place to place. To find out more please look at the American Association for Higher Education (AAHE) resource pages on electronic portfolios: http://aahe.ital.utexas.edu/electronicportfolios/ (accessed April 2003).

GIVING FEEDBACK TO STUDENTS: FORMATIVE ASSESSMENT

Ask any of your students 'What helps you to learn?' and the vast majority will include 'getting helpful feedback' towards the top of their list. It is central to how learners develop and improve their skills and understanding in all aspects of study. It is, however, time consuming and expensive in tutor time. Many tutors may spend as much time marking and giving feedback as they do in class.

Do your students appreciate the value of your comments and marks? Do you encourage them to make the most of your feedback?

Feedback isn't always useful

For some students, the grade is everything and they may give the comments and suggestions written on their work, or made by their tutor, only a glancing thought. This may be because the topic has 'been and gone' for them and that feedback on the specifics of the topic has lost its relevance. It may be because the feedback arrives with the students too long after they did the work and the students have forgotten what they did and moved on to the next part of the course. The students may be locked into a 'task completion' frame of mind often associated with a surface approach to learning (see the series web site at www.routledgefalmer.com/series/KGETHE for more about approaches to learning). So they were originally motivated to get the essay written or the talk given and were less concerned with the learning taking place. In this situation the feedback you offer will be detached from the students' own goals and, therefore, likely to have very little impact. It maybe that the feedback is given in such a way as to discourage the student engaging with it. The feedback may make the student feel discouraged, embarrassed, angry, frustrated, misunderstood or stupid because of the way in which it was delivered. A student feeling like this is more likely to want to quickly file the work away rather than review it closely and think about what they might do differently next time.

189

Effective feedback

Feedback is effective only if the student can 'hear it', 'understand it' and then, most importantly, 'act upon it in order to improve what they do'. So the clever pearls of wisdom the assessor writes on an essay are worthless if the student does not consider them. It is, therefore, crucially important that as much care and thought is given to 'how' the students will receive the feedback as 'what' is actually said.

In all matters of learning the emphasis should be on the learner and not on the tutor – in this case the emphasis is on the receiver of feedback rather than the giver. When you formatively assess a student's work, you are not carrying out an exercise in academic criticism but you are trying to help somebody to 'do it better next time'. When you are giving feedback on a student's oral presentation, you are not trying to list every error they made but to build their confidence and highlight one or two areas that they will be able to work on and improve.

Good feedback is . . .

Timely

Feedback should be delivered soon after the work was originally carried out. This is often stipulated by an institution, e.g. 'All written work must be marked and returned within two weeks'. Or 'Give oral feedback on presentations immediately afterwards and pass the presenter a copy of your completed assessment form at the end of the session'.

Specific

Feedback should be clearly focused on specific aspects of the work explaining why something is good, bad or indifferent, e.g. 'The talk was very good . . . because the presenter maintained eye contact with the group, used clear visual aids and used a range of appropriate examples'.

Owned

Personal to the tutor and personal to the student, the feedback you give is your view and it is directed towards a student who you know in the bigger context, that is you know how this work compares with their previous work, e.g. 'I thought you rushed the conclusion of your presentation, and I remember you did this last time. So I think you should rethink your time planning and see that it is taking you a bit longer than you are expecting?'

Prioritized

Feedback should be focused on the most important points in order to have the biggest beneficial impact. Know your students, their personality, their level of development and their concerns, what strengths and weaknesses are the most important for them now. It is easy to overwhelm with good intentions.

Constructive

Feedback should be concerned with improvement. The tutor should try to convey why something is problematic or successful in the work and indicate how the problem can be resolved or the strength embedded or developed, e.g. 'You are beginning to reference a wide range of sources in your essays, which is excellent. However, some of your references are not presented consistently. Take a look at the paper we used in class and check the way in which the authors reference both journal articles and chapters in edited books.'

Justifiable

Feedback should be defendable; the tutor can explain their judgements and comments in relation to the learning outcomes and the assessment criteria for the work. This is about being fair and consistent and avoiding bias.

Respectful

Feedback should be delivered kindly and with consideration of feelings. Feedback should not undermine the students but help them to develop and grow in their disciplines. Speak (or write) as you would like to be spoken to.

Building

Feedback starts with the students' current level of understanding or ability and seeks to encourage them to develop further. Indicate what the next level looks like in terms that they can understand, e.g. 'Your analysis was well executed. Can you now suggest any improvements to the original method or make any recommendations for future studies?'

Linked to formative and summative assessments

Feedback should be integrated with the marks awarded and the summative assessments that the students will take. Feedback comments should be in harmony with the marks or grade awarded. The formative feedback assessments should clearly link with the final summative assessments to be taken by the students by valuing the same skills and attributes, e.g.

> Your essay was nearly 700 words over the word limit and in the exam you will only have three-quarters of an hour to write your essays so trying to write more succinctly and concisely will be important.

Above all, *good feedback is encouraging.*

How to give feedback

It is just as important to say 'That is good, keep doing that' as it is to point out difficulties or weaknesses in the work. In giving feedback the tutor should try to be balanced. The Open University encourages its tutors to balance positive and negative feedback (Baume 1998) through the following structure.

- *Start with positive comments:* there is always something, and usually lots of things, that the tutor can praise and comment on positively.
- *Comment on specific weaknesses in the work and provide guidance on how they can be improved or corrected:* remember to prioritize and focus comments to help the student address the most significant shortfalls in his or her work.
- *Finish with an encouraging summary:* conclude with the main points that the student should seek to address, while noting the strengths of the work and communicated with a positive and encouraging attitude. The intention is that the outcome of receiving feedback is that the student feels motivated to try to improve what he or she does and has clear information on which to act.

This structure is sometimes referred to as the 'Feedback sandwich'.

Giving feedback may be part of a more iterative and interactive process, for example, giving oral feedback to a student who has just given a presentation. In this case it may be helpful to both the students and the tutor to start by asking the students themselves what they thought of their own presentation. Asking students to report one thing they would do differently, and one thing that they would keep the same if they were asked to repeat their presentation, can be a way of inviting self-reflection and evaluation. In practice the tutor is likely to find that the students are very willing to criticize their own work but less willing to point out its strengths. The role of the tutor is therefore one of highlighting good points and minimizing the harsh self-criticism.

Oral and written feedback

If the tutor is able to present feedback face-to-face with the student or deliver oral feedback, this opens up the possibility of further dialogue. The student can ask for clarification and discuss the implication of the points raised. The tutor can invite the student to paraphrase what was said to him or her and so check understanding. The tutor may also ask for the student's reactions to the feedback: 'Do you agree?' 'What actions do you intend to make?'

Giving verbal feedback undoubtedly has advantages but the tutor does need to consider the following:

- *Student confidentiality:* will the student react differently if given private or public feedback? It is often beneficial in a collaborative learning situation, such as a tutorial, to share feedback so that students can learn from their own feedback and that offered to their colleagues too. However, some students may prefer difficult feedback to be given more privately.
- *Student tolerance:* some students may feel very uncomfortable if given 'too much' praise or given 'too many' suggestions for improvement. What is 'too much' will be different for each student and will vary between cultures. Therefore, the tutor needs to be sensitive and particularly aware of body language that indicates tension and unease.
- *Student misunderstanding:* any purely verbal form of communication is more prone to confusions of comprehension or interpretation. Students who speak English as a second language may be particularly vulnerable here.

193

- *Student memory:* it is unlikely that all that was said will be accurately remembered. If a student is anxious or euphoric (having given and finished a talk) it is to be expected that he or she will not be able to take on board and retain all that was said in feedback. A tutor may even suspect a student of having a 'selective memory', conveniently forgetting the 'less welcome' elements of the feedback.

- *Tutor memory:* the tutor should keep a record of the feedback given to the students in order to monitor progress and see development. Even in a small group keeping track of what was said to whom is difficult. Some institutions may also require tutors to maintain a log of the feedback they have given to their students.

For these reasons a combination of both oral and written feedback is probably the most useful form of feedback to have.

The students themselves can be encouraged to make a written record of the oral feedback they have received and pass a copy to the tutor. Alternatively the tutor can produce a 'feedback form' which can be completed, discussed with the students and kept as a record.

Such pro-formas may invite open comment under general headings of strengths and weaknesses (Table 11.7) or be more detailed in their use of specific assessment criteria and grading scales (Table 11.8).

Asking students to give feedback to each other

Table 11.9 shows that such a feedback form can also be readily used by students in order to give each other feedback too. This does need to be carefully introduced and explained to ensure that everyone understands the nature of effective feedback and that the students are considerate and sensitive to each other's feelings.

Such an approach is most commonly used to give feedback on presentations and posters however; it can be very beneficial to ask students to swap their essays or reports and to give each other feedback. Tutors attending workshops report that maximum benefit is derived if they take time to explain why they are asking students to give each other feedback, if they provide clear guidance on how to evaluate the work and if they ask the students to focus on how work is structured and presented rather than on the quality and accuracy of the information included.

TABLE 11.7 Feedback assessment sheet used to give open comments to a student presenter

Feedback sheet

Overall I thought your talk was

Excellent   Good   Adequate   Poor   Inadequate

Three things I really liked were:

■

■

■

Three things that I think could be improved were:

■

■

■

TABLE 11.8 Giving feedback to peers who are giving an oral presentation

Feedback form
Please provide constructive feedback under the following headings. Remember to highlight strengths as well as weaknesses. Aim to be constructive.

The structure and organization of the talk

The use of audio-visual aids

Communication skills (use of the voice and body language)

Interaction with and involvement of the seminar group

Additional comments

TABLE 11.9 A feedback pro-forma used to give feedback to student seminar presenters or facilitators

Assessment criteria	1 Excellent	2	3	4	5 Poor
Clarity of structure					
Appropriateness of content and quality of arguments					
Verbal and non-verbal communication					
Use of visual aids and handouts					
Interaction with the audience and response to questions					

General comments

 **FURTHER READING**

Boud, D., Cohen, R. and Sampson, J. (2001) 'Peer learning and assessment', in D. Boud, R. Cohen and J. Sampson, *Peer Learning in Higher Education: Learning from and with Each Other*, London: Kogan Page.

Brown, S. (1998) *Peer Assessment in Practice*, SEDA Paper 102, Birmingham: Staff and Educational Development Association.

Doran, S., Durston, C., Fletcher, A. and Longmore, J. (2000), 'Assessing students in seminars: an evaluation of current practice', in A. Booth and P. Hyland (eds) *The Practice of University History Teaching*, Manchester: Manchester University Press.

Knight, P. (ed.) (1995) *Assessment for Learning in Higher Education*, London: Kogan Page.

USEFUL WEB SITES

http://www.brookes.ac.uk/services/ocsd/firstwords/fw26.html Oxford Centre for Staff and Learning Development (OCSLD), Oxford Brookes University, First Words web site gives quick advice and guidance on the assessment of group work (accessed 8 June 2003).

http://www.iml.uts.edu.au/learnteach/groupwork/unit6.html Institutute for Interactive Media and Learning, University of Technology Sydney, web site provides a comprehensive look at assessing group work but focuses on a number of alternative approaches and outlines the strengths and weaknesses of each (accessed 8 June 2003).

http://www.lancs.ac.uk/palatine/topics/group.htm Many of the LTSN web sites have space dedicated to the assessment of group work and teamworking (accessed 8 June 2003).

http://www.wcer.wisc.edu/nise/cl1/CL/default.asp The Collaborative Learning web pages offer well-referenced articles on many aspects of small group learning including group based assessment (accessed 8 June 2003).

References

Albanese, M. A. and Mitchell, S. (1993) 'Problem-based learning: a review of literature on its outcomes and implementation issues', *Academic Medicine* 68(1): 52–81.

Annis, L. F. (1983) 'The processes and effects of peer tutoring', *Human Learning* 2: 39–47.

Armstrong, R., Percival, F. and Saunders, D. (1994) *The Simulation and Gaming Yearbook Volume 2*, London: Kogan Page.

ASTER Project (Assisting Small-group Teaching through Electronic Resources) *Small Group Teaching and C&IT*, http://cti-psy.york.ac.uk/aster/ (accessed 12 June 2003).

Atherton, J. S. (2002) *Approaches to Study, 'Deep' and 'Surface'*, http://www.dmu.ac.uk/~jamesa/learning/deepsurf.htm (accessed 12 June 2003).

Ausubel, D. P. (1968) *Educational Psychology: A Cognitive View*, New York: Holt, Rinehart and Winston.

Bargh, J. A. and Schul, Y. (1980) 'On the cognitive benefits of teaching', *Journal of Educational Psychology* 72(5): 593–604.

Barker, P. (2002) 'On being an online tutor', *Innovations in Education and Teaching International* 3(1): 3–13.

Barrows H. S. (1986) 'A taxonomy of problem-based learning methods', *Medical Education* 20: 481–6.

Barrows, H. S. and Tamblyn, R. M. (1980) *Problem Based Learning: An Approach to Medical Education*, New York: Springer.

Baume, D. (1998) *Marking and Giving Feedback: Practice Guide 4*, H851 Teaching in Higher Education, Institute of Educational Technology, Milton Keynes: The Open University.

Baume, D. and Baume, C. (1996) *Learning to Teaching: Running Tutorials and Seminars – Training Materials for Research Students*, Oxford: Oxford Centre for Staff Development.

Becher, T. (1989) *Academic Tribes and Territories, Intellectual Enquiry and the Cultures of Disciplines*, Buckingham: Society for Research into Higher Education and Open University Press.

Belbin, R. M. (1993) *Team Roles at Work*, Oxford: Butterworth-Heinemann.

Benner, P. (1984) *From Novice to Expert: Excellence and Power in Clinical Nursing*, London: Addison Wesley.

Berkson, L. (1993) 'Problem-based learning: have the expectations been met?' *Academic Medicine* 68(10): S79–S88.

Biggs, J. (1999) *Teaching for Quality Learning in Higher Education*, Buckingham: Society for Research into Higher Education and Open University Press.

Bloom, B. S. (1956, 1964) *Taxonomy of Educational Objectives*, 2 vols, New York: Longmans Green.

Booth, A. (1996) 'Assessing group work', in A. Booth and P. Hyland (eds) *History in Higher Education*, Oxford: Blackwell.

Boud, D. (1995) *Enhancing Learning through Self-assessment*, London: Kogan Page.

Boud, D. and Feletti, G. (eds) (1997) *The Challenge of Problem Based Learning*, 2nd edn, London: Kogan Page.

Boud, D., Cohen, R. and Sampson, J. (2001) *Peer Learning in Higher Education: Learning from and with Each Other*, London: Kogan Page.

Bramley, M. (1996) 'How to make boring material interesting', in D. Allan (ed.) *In at the Deep End: First Experiences of University Teaching*, Innovation in Higher Education Series, Lancaster: Lancaster University.

Brookfield, S. D. (1987) *Developing Critical Thinkers: Challenging Adults to Explore Alternative Ways of Thinking and Acting*, Buckingham: Open University Press.

Brown, G. (2004) *How Students Learn*, http://www.routledgefalmer.com/series/KGETHE

Brown, G., Bull, B. and Pendlebury, M. (1997) *Assessing Student Learning in Higher Education*, London and New York: Routledge.

Brown, S. (1998) *Peer Assessment in Practice*, SEDA Paper 102, Birmingham: Staff and Educational Development Association.

Burke, J. (1989) *Competency-Based Education and Training*, London and New York: Falmer.

Buzan, T. (1993) *The Mind Map Book: How to Use Radiant Thinking to Maximise your Brain's Untapped Potential*, London: Penguin.

Calaprice, A. (2000) *The Expanded Quotable Einstein*, Princeton, NJ: Princeton University Press.

Carin, A. A. and Sund, R. B. (1971) *Developing Questioning Techniques: A Self-concept Approach*, Columbus, OH: Charles E. Merrill.

Chin, P. (2004) *Using C&IT to Support Teaching*, London: RoutledgeFalmer.

Clack, G. B. (1994) 'Medical graduates evaluate the effectiveness of their education', *Medical Education* 28: 418–31.

Coles, C. (1991) 'Is problem-based learning the only way?', in D. Boud and G. Felletti (eds) *The Challenge of Problem-based Learning*, London: Kogan Page.

Cross, K. P. (1981) *Adults as Learners*, San Francisco, CA: Jossey-Bass.

Cross, K. P. (1999) 'How to find out whether students are learning what you are teaching', in J. D. Nyquist, R. D. Abbott, D. H. Wulff and J. Sprague (eds) *Preparing the Professoriate of Tomorrow to Teach: Selected Readings in TA Training*, Dubuque, IA: Kendall/Hunt.

Dearing, R. (1997) *Higher Education in the Learning Society*, Report of the National Committee of Inquiry into Higher Education, London: HMSO.

Dennick, R. and Exley, K. (1998) 'Teaching and learning in groups and teams', *Biochemical Education* 26: 111–15.

Dewey, J. (1916) *Democracy and Education*, New York: Macmillan.

Dewey, J. (1938) *Experience and Education*, New York: Macmillan.

Doran, S., Durston, C., Fletcher, A. and Longmore, J. (2000) 'Assessing students in seminars: an evaluation of current practice', in A. Booth and P. Hyland (eds) *The Practice of University History Teaching*, Manchester: Manchester University Press.

Duffy, T. M., Dueber, B. and Hawley, C. L. (1999) 'Critical thinking in a distributed environment: a pedagogical base for the design of conferencing systems', in C. J. Bonk and K. S. King (eds) *Electronic Collaborators: Learner-centered Technologies for Literacy, Apprenticeship, and Discourse*, Mahwah, NJ: Lawrence Erlbaum.

Elwyn, G., Greenhalgh, T. and Macfarlane, F. (2001) *Groups: A Guide to Small group Work in Healthcare, Management, Education and Research*, London: Radcliffe Medical Press.

Engel, C. E. (1991) 'Not just a method but a way of learning', in D. Boud and G. Felletti (eds) *The Challenge of Problem-based Learning*, London: Kogan Page.

English National Board (1998) 'Developments in the use of an evidence and/or enquiry based approach in nursing, midwifery and health visiting programmes of education', http://www.enb.org.uk/evidpub.htm (accessed 12 June 2003).

Entwistle, N., Thompson, S. and Tait, H. (1992) *Guidelines for Promoting Learning in Higher Education*, Edinburgh: Centre for Research on Learning and Instruction, University of Edinburgh.

Exley, K. (2001) *BEATL Evalution Report, Case Study 8, Concrete Images*, Leicester: Department of Architecture, De Montfort University.

Falchikov, N. (2001) *Learning Together: Peer Tutoring in Higher Education*, London: RoutledgeFalmer.

Festinger, L. (1957) *A Theory of Cognitive Dissonance*, Stanford, CA: Stanford University Press.

Fitts, P. and Posner, M. (1967) *Human Performance*, Belmont, CA: Brooks/Cole.

Froebel, F. W. (1886) *The Education of Man*, trans. J. Jarvis, New York: A. Lovell.

George, J. H. and Doto, F. X. (2001) 'A simple five-step method for teaching clinical skills', *Family Medicine* 33: 577–8.

Haines, C. (2004) *Assessing Students' Written Work*, London: RoutledgeFalmer.

Hayler, R. and Funnel, M. (1998) 'Proctoring for philosophy students', in

J. Dolan and A. J. Castley (eds) *Students Supporting Students*, SEDA Paper 105, Birmingham: Staff and Educational Development Association.

Heron, J. (1989) *The Facilitators' Handbook*, London: Kogan Page.

Higher Education Funding Council for England (HEFCE) (2001) *Strategies for Widening Participation in Higher Education*, Guide 01/30, http://www.hefce.ac.uk/pubs/hefce/2001/01_36.htm (accessed 9 June 2003).

Hoadley, C. M. and Bell, P. (1996) 'Web for your head: the design of digital resources to enhance lifelong learning', *D-LIB Magazine*, September; see also http://sensemaker.stanford.edu/

Holsbrick-Engels, G. (1994) 'Visions of Dutch corporate trainers on role playing', in R. Armstrong, F. Percival and D. Saunders (eds) *The Simulation and Gaming Yearbook Volume 2*, London: Kogan Page.

Honey, P. (1982) *The Manual of Learning Styles*, Maidenhead: Honey and Mumford.

Jaques, D. (2000) *Learning in Groups: A Handbook for Improving Group Work*, 3rd edn, London: Kogan Page.

Johnson, D. W. and Johnson, R. T. (1985) 'The internal dynamics of co-operative learning groups', in R. Slavin, S. Sharon, S. Kagan, R. Hertz-Lazarowitz, C. Webb and R. Schmuck (eds) *Learning to Cooperate, Cooperation to Learn*, New York and London: Plenum.

Kipling, R. (1912) *Just So Stories for Children*, Garden City, NY: The Country Life Press.

Klemm, W. R. (1998) 'Eight ways to get students more engaged in online conferences', http://www.thejournal.com/magazine/vault/A1997A.cfm (accessed 19 October 2003).

Knight, P. (ed.) (1995) *Assessment for Learning in Higher Education*, London: Kogan Page.

Knight, P. (2002) *Being a Teacher in Higher Education*, Buckingham: Society for Research into Higher Education and Open University Press.

Knowles, M. (1990 [1973]) *The Adult Learner: A Neglected Species*, Houston, TX: Gulf.

Kolb, D. (1984) *Experiential Learning*, Englewood Cliffs, NJ: Prentice Hall.

Lewin, K. (1952) *Field Theory in Social Science*, London: Tavistock.

Maguire, P., Fairbairn, S. and Fletcher, C. (1986) 'Consultation skills of young doctors', *British Medical Journal* 292: 1573–8.

Malseed, J. (1994) 'Forty-eight warm-ups for group work', in R. Armstrong, F. Percival and D. Saunders (eds) *The Simulation and Gaming Yearbook Volume 2*, London: Kogan Page.

Maslow, A. (1954) *Motivation and Personality*, New York: Harper and Brothers.

Maslow, A. (1968) *Towards a Psychology of Being*, New York: Van Nostrand.

Miller, G. E. (1990) 'The assessment of clinical skills/competence/performance', *Academic Medicine* 65(9): 563–7.

Moon, J. (2001) *Short Courses and Workshops*, London: Kogan Page.

Newman, M. (2003) 'A pilot systematic review and meta-analysis on the effectiveness of Problem Based Learning (PDF)', Middlesex University, http://www.hebes.mdx.ac.uk/teaching/Research/PEPBL/index.htm (accessed 25 July 2003).

Nicholson, T. and Ellis, G. (2000) 'Assessing group work to develop collaborative learning', in A. Booth and P. Hyland (eds) *The Practice of University History Teaching*, Manchester: Manchester University Press.

Norman, G. and Schmidt, H. (1992) 'The psychological basis of problem-based learning: a review of the evidence', *Academic Medicine* 67(9): 557–64.

Northedge, A. and the H851/HH851 course team (1998) *Practice Guide 1: Teaching in Groups*, OU Series H851 Teaching in HE: theory and evidence, Milton Keynes: The Open University.

Osborne, A. F. (1957) *Applied Imagination*, New York: Scribner's.

Phillips, D. C. (2000) 'An opinionated account of the constructivist landscape', in D. C. Phillips (ed.) *Constructivism in Education: Opinions and Second Opinions on Controversial Issues*, Chicago: University of Chicago Press.

Pinker, S. (2002) *The Blank Slate*, London: Allen Lane Press.

Quality Assurance Agency for Higher Education (QAA) (1999) *Code of Practice for the Assurance of Academic Quality and Standards in Higher Education: Students with Disabilities*, http://www.qaa.ac.uk/public/COP/COPswd/contents.htm (accessed 12 June 2003).

Quinn, F. M. (2000) *Principles and Practice of Nurse Education*, Cheltenham: Nelson Thornes.

Raaheim, K. (1991) 'The first examinations at university', in K. Raaheim, J. Wankowski and J. Radford (eds) *Helping Students to Learn: Teaching, Counselling, Research*, Buckingham: Society for Research into Higher Education and Open University Press.

Ramsden, P. (1984) 'The context of learning in academic departments', in D. Hounsell and N. Entwistle (eds) *The Experience of Learning*, 2nd edn, Edinburgh: Scottish Academic Press.

Roberts, V. C. (1994) *Tutor Resource Manual: Tutoring Students in the Community College*, Virginia, MN: Arrowhead Community Colleges.

Rogers, C. (1983) *Freedom to Learn for the 80s*, Columbus, OH: Charles E. Merrill.

Rousseau, J. J. (1762) *Emile, or on Education*, trans. A. Bloom, New York: Basic Books.

Ryan, S., Freeman, H., Scott, B. and Patel, D. (2000) *The Virtual University: The Internet and Resource-Based Learning*, London: Kogan Page.

Salmon, G. (1997) 'On the line: developing conferencing within a distance learning management education context: training the tutors', Milton Keynes: Open University, http://oubs.ac.uk/gilly

Sampson, J. and Cohen, R. (2001) 'Strategies for peer learning: some examples', in D. Boud, R. Cohen and J. Sampson (eds) *Peer Learning in Higher Education: Learning from and with Each Other*, London: Kogan Page.

Savin-Baden, M. (2000) *Problem-based Learning in Higher Education: Untold*

Stories, Buckingham: Society for Research into Higher Education and Open University Press.

Schmidt, H. G. (1983) 'Problem-based learning: rationale and description', *Medical Education* 17: 11–16.

Schön, D. (1983) *The Reflective Practitioner*, London: Jossey-Bass.

Schön, D. (1987) *Educating the Reflective Practitioner*, London: Jossey-Bass.

Shephard, C. (2003) E-learning's Greatest Hits, Above and Beyond Ltd, UK.

Simpson, J. S. (1966) *The Classification of Educational Objectives: Psychomotor Domain*, Office of Education Project 5-85-104, Urbana, IL: University of Illinois.

Slavin, R., Sharon, S., Kagan, S., Hertz-Lazarowitz, R., Webb, C. and Schmuck, R. (eds) (1985) *Learning to Cooperate, Cooperation to Learn*, New York and London: Plenum Press.

Tansley, C. and Bryson, C. (2000) 'Virtual seminars: a viable substitute for traditional approaches?', *Innovations in Education and Training International* 27(4): 323–35.

Van Ments, M. (1989) *The Effective Use of Role Play*, London: Kogan Page.

Vernon, D. T. A. and Blake, R. L. (1993) 'Does problem-based learning work? A meta-analysis of evaluative research', *Academic Medicine* 69(7): 550–63.

Walton, H. J. and Matthews, M. B. (1989) 'Essentials of problem based learning', *Medical Education* 23: 542–58.

Waterfield, J. and West, B. (2002) *SENDA Compliance in Higher Education*, South West Academic Network for Disability Support (SWANDS), University of Plymouth and HEFCE.

Westberg, J. and Jason, H. (1996) *Fostering Learning in Small Groups: A Practical Guide*, New York: Springer.

Wilkie, K. (2000) 'The nature of problem-based learning', in S. Glen and K. Wilkie (eds) *Problem-based Learning in Nursing*, London: Macmillan Press.

World Bank (1993) *World Development Report 1993: Investing in Health*, Oxford: Oxford University Press.

World Health Organization (WHO) (1993) *Increasing the Relevance of Education for Health Professionals*, Report of a WHO Study Group on Problem Solving Education for Health Professionals, Technical Report Series 838, Geneva: WHO.

Zimmer, R. and Alexander, G. (1996) 'The Rogerian interface: for open warm empathy in computer-mediated communication', *Innovation in Education and Training International* 33(1): 13–21.

Index

Page numbers in *italics* refer to figures and tables.

preparation 13–15; whole-group 98; workshops 137
prior learning: activation of 22–3, 40, 41, 85–6; 'life experience' 161
probing questions 44–6
problem groups 27–31
problem-based learning (PBL): curriculum 77–8, 79, 89; definition 76–7; educational rationale for 84–7; evidence for effectiveness 89–90; examples from different disciplines 91–2, 141–3; facilitator 88–9; setting up a course 89; seven-step process 80–4; tutorial 80
process focus 3–4
proctorials 95–6; philosophy 106–7; see also tutorials
professional attitudes to learning 32–3, 87
professional development see continuing development
'professional' skills 111
progress development files (PDFs) see personal development profiles (PDPs)
progressive tasks 153
prompting questions 45
psychomotor/practical skills 111–17
'pyramiding' pairs 61

Qualifications and Curriculum Authority (QCA) 110, 163
Quality Assurance Agency for Higher Education (QAA) 7–8, 124–5
questions/questioning 24–5; categories of 41–6; facilitation through 39–47; function of 39–41; process 46–7; student-led seminars 99
quizzes: computer-aided assessment (CAA) 122; 'pre-test' 55–6; student-led seminars 100–1

Ramsden, P. 107
reading assignments 97
'reasonable adjustment', disabled students 162–3, 164–6
Recommendation 21 (Dearing Report) 109–10
records: PDPs 11, 22, 124–5; written 25, 103
redirecting questions 46
'reflecting back' 38
'reflecting-in-action' 6
reflective practice/practitioner 5, 6, 87
refocusing discussions 129
reforming 147; trainee GP workshop 146–8
'regular' groups 26–7
resources 15; C&IT 120–1; disabled students 165–6, 167; independent/additional learning, PBL 83–4; paper-based 63–4; workshops 137
responding 38–9
reviewing 41, 84
risk levels in activities 53–5
Rogers, Carl 33, 34–5, 46, 88
role-play 66–9, 74; fish-bowling 65, 66
room location 137
room size 18
rounds 56–7
Ryan, S. et al. 130

Savin-Baden, M. 86, 90
'scenarios', PBL 77, 78, 83, 85, 91–2
Schmidt, H. G. 80
Schön, Donald 6, 87
seating arrangements 17–18; circular 53–4
self-actualization 34–5
self-assessment 175–6, 186–7
self-selected groups 153